Selling Your Business

A Quick Reference Guide

A Fast Track to Understanding the Process of Selling Your
Small to Medium Sized Business (under £50M)

Ken Gorman

TABLE OF CONTENTS

FORWARD

This book is dedicated to the brave souls who start and run Small/Medium-Sized Enterprises (SMEs). This usually means they are under £50M in Enterprise Value and run by one or two owners.

Most of these heroes have worked all hours and weathered the ups and downs of the business cycle to get to a point in their life where they can see the light at the end of the tunnel, a time when they can take a well-deserved break and think about retirement. And so begins the business exit process.

The purpose of this book is to help business owners have at least a high-level understanding of all the aspects of the business sale process to actively participate with the advisors rather than potentially be at their mercy.

For most people selling a business is a HUGE life event. It can be as significant as getting married or having children and is often more complicated. The process of selling a business most often arises due to a desire to retire, which is one of life's major transitions. Often a business is the most valuable asset a person owns and the sale will fund this retirement. So, in addition to the emotional side, selling their business may be the most important financial transaction of their lives.

Most business owners have spent years working to become the best in their fields and have had many years of success as a result. When it came time to leave their businesses, we found that these same people had no idea how the process worked, how to maximise the value of their business, how long it would take and how to manage their own wealth as it related to their business to name a few.

This book arose as I perceived a need to educate potential business Sellers on all the aspects of this important event. I have done 100s of first meetings with potential clients as a Sell Side Merger and Acquisition (M&A) Advisor and it always amazes me how little people understand about the aspects involved in the business exit process.

Although there are many advisors who will happily assist in these areas, our experience is that the business owner is often left confused as different advisors give different views and/or are at the mercy of poor advisors just chasing fees. One antidote for this is some basic education on the different aspects of the business exit process in order for them to participate intelligently with the advisors and sleep well at night, knowing they got a good deal throughout the process.

Exiting your business may be one of the most important things you do in your life. Understanding the fundamentals to participate with the advisors rather than be at their mercy along with good planning, execution and the right help ensures a rewarding outcome.

Ken Gorman, CM&AA

Merger & Acquisitions Advisor

Chapter 1
When is the Right Time to
Sell Your Business?

I have had hundreds of discussions with business owners who ask a very natural question: when is a good time to sell my business? The answer most people expect from a Sale Side M&A Advisor is some commentary on finances and how much they need to sell for, the state of the market, a discussion about what improvements they could make and the impact on valuation, etc.

However, what I have found consistently in speaking with 100s of Sellers is that those that are ready have a sort of 'switch' that has gone off inside of them. I have learned to ascertain very early whether this switch has gone off and they have a genuine feeling it is time to move on. Many things in our life are like this like when to get married, when to sell a house, change jobs, etc. and selling a business is no different in most cases.

If this switch has gone off, usually it is important that they respond to it and start the business sale process. There are many reasons for this including the fact they will generally suffer from a lack of inspiration and drive if they don't start a sale process and the business will decline. We have all seen many cases of this where the Seller puts it off, often because their accountant is telling them how much money they can make, and the business declines taking a huge chunk of valuation with it.

There is another group of people that the switch has not totally gone off but they can see it coming in the next 3-5 years and know they need to start preparing. This group of people can be worked with to make the changes necessary in the business to maximise valuation and make it easy to sell (these are covered in a later chapter). This group generally does not feel ready to sell today and still has enough inspiration left to drive the business for the next 3-5 years.

So our experience is that if a business owner knows in their heart it is time to sell, it usually is. There are exceptions to this which generally happen when a business will not sell for enough to fund the individual's retirement for example.

Or it could be the financials are down and need to recover or they may have a partner who is not ready. There are many more examples of structural issues that prevent a person from selling their business even though they might be ready. But for most, they know it is time to begin and a good M&A Advisor can help them engage with the journey.

CHAPTER 2

TYPICAL TIME SCALES

How long it takes to sell a business and when should I start planning are common questions. There are several answers to this question but one way to break it down is into three basic categories of business owners who are thinking about selling:

- **Immediate – 1 or 2 Years to Exit -** These business owners need to look at starting the business sale process now as it can take a year to sell and another year to exit completely in many cases. They probably do not have time to make fundamental changes to the business. They should think about contacting a Sell Side M&A Advisor to begin the process.
- **Medium Term - 3-5 Years to Exit –** These business owners have time to make changes in the business to improve valuations and make the business more salable. They can work with business acceleration/optimisation specialists to improve EBITDA, make sure they are replaceable, improve books and records, etc. They can also work with personal financial planners and tax advisors to make plans for their personal cash flow and wealth management.
- **Longer Term – Over 5 Years or Indefinite –** The dynamics and approach are the same as the 3-5 year category. The difference is that the 'switch' inside of them that is triggering them to think about exit has generally not manifested so their motivation and perspective may be different. Often there is more soul searching about where they want to be long-term and a broader business

direction rather than motivation for a very focused, concrete plan to prepare the business for sale in a specified time period.

When asked "How long does it take to sell a business?" I frequently respond with the old adage, 'How long is a piece of string?'

This is not a particularly helpful answer, but it is at least an honest one. When new to the business sales process, I quickly learned that the financial data the Seller makes available provides some clues to a possible timescale but a multitude of other factors will impact the length of a particular business sale process.

Average Timescales and Statistics for the Actual Business Sale Process

The first thing to understand is a few statistics to have a feel for how the business sale process actually pans out in reality:

8.2 Months - The International Business Brokers Association (IBBA) states that based on their research, the average business sells in 8.2 months. (It is important to note that these are averages so for larger, more complex businesses the time can actually be much longer).

75% Post Heads of Terms/Letter of Intent Drop Out Rate - The IBBA also reports that 75% of business sale transactions fall through 'after' offers are agreed upon between Buyer and Seller during the due diligence and contract phase. Yes, mathematically this means each Buyer on average will have three false starts (the fourth one wins) before getting to the end if they are even in the percentage of businesses that complete a successful transaction.

12% Sell Who Go It Alone on Internet Sites - Another important statistic is that business owners who attempt to sell their business on their own through internet sites are only successful about 12% of the time.

95% of Buyers Who Enquire Never Buy From Us - We mirror that by our own statistic which is that 98% that enquire about a business will never buy one from us. (The business Sellers we represent probably see 5% of the Buyers that enquire about their business as we have a multi-layered screening process).

60% - 80% of Businesss That Go Up for Sell, Dont Sell - This is a statistic that is often quoted by business brokerage firms and probably has some truth to it. However, the statistic is skewed by High Street businesses (fast food, beauty etc.) that are often harder to sell. Also, often a Seller will put the busines on the market and withdraw it if they cant get enough money or for personal reasons. But it makes the point...selling a business is hard and not a guarantee in the same way as selling a property might be. For those good, profitable business with solid books and processes that do want to sell, the main reason they don't sell is a) lack of a sophisticated buyer outreach program and b) lack of good process management during the due diligence/contract phase as above. (Fortunately a good M&A Advisor can mitigate both of these issues).

Further Comments on the Business Sale Process Timescales

The 8.2 months previously quoted needs to be taken with a pinch of salt as this will include all businesses in the SME category, many of which could be quite small and the process happens more quickly. For comparison, let's examine a fish and chip shop on the high street alongside a complex manufacturing company with several sites, maybe some of them not even in the UK.

One would think that the fish and chips would sell faster than the complex machine shop. However, there is another factor which is that not all businesses even sell. If a business is not very sellable in the first place (i.e. it may have low profits or no profits) there is a long period during which the owner adjusts to the situation. It takes time to become accustomed to the fact that, if they want to sell their business at all, it will be for a very low price. This all adds elapsed time and influences the statistics of course.

On the other hand, a complex machine shop with excellent books and records (see a later chapter on the importance of this), great EBITDA, that is priced right with a highly motivated Seller can find a Buyer within 2 weeks of listing.

Yes, the due diligence and legal process will always take a few months longer than a fish and chip shop transaction but the deal will be completed in 6 months. The fish and chip business with poor books and records, overpriced with an owner who was not that motivated to sell will still be on the market. We could still be marketing this business 18 months later when the owner finally decides he really does want to sell and drops the price.

The motivation of the Seller is another huge factor in how quickly a business sells. A business owner that is ready to retire has made a plan. They understand that by the time they sell the business (8.2 months for argument's sake) and work in the business for another year, they are 20 months away from their daily appointment with the golf course and it cannot come soon enough!

This type of Seller will price the business right, put the work in to get through due diligence in a timely fashion and make the compromises and adjustments necessary to get the deal done. In contrast, with an unmotivated Seller who is just testing the market, there are just too many obstacles and the chances of getting to the end of the process are very low in the first place.

With that in mind, if the first Buyer that makes an offer were to get to closing, here are roughly the timescales we normally see:

1. Packaging and submitting for marketing - 2 Weeks
2. Viewings and meeting Buyers - 1-2 months
3. Offers and negotiation to get to Heads of Terms (HOT) after Buyer identified - 2 weeks
4. Due Diligence - 2 months (this varies greatly so just a ballpark average)

5. Contracts and eliminating contingencies including funding - 2 months (this also varies greatly so just a ballpark average)

So if everything went according to plan and the first Buyer completed, the process on the above timescales would take 6 months. We have completed transactions that were 4 months from listing to closing day and the owner was on his sailboat full-time by month 6. It really does depend on the Buyer, Seller and the nature of the business.

There are many things that can slow the process down. Here are a few of the major ones we find:

- Seller not having financials ready or waiting on a year-end and then for the financials to be complete
- Buyers getting funding (contingent on the point above)
- Lease transfer and getting the landlord on board (generally requires paying landlord's solicitor fee, references and getting their approval)
- Getting franchisor approval (many will require the Buyer to go to training and be certified as well as pay a transfer fee)
- Slow legal council (this is a big issue that needs to be managed and can create weeks of delay towards the end of the process)

There is one final factor in both how long it takes to move through this process and increasing the chance of getting to the end of a successful close which is good process management. There are many moving parts, the parties have dozens of items they need to produce and do and there are many external people involved in the process which all need to be managed in a sort of concert.

The key to the optimisation of this process is a good M&A Advisor with experience in doing many transactions. They will have well-honed systems that they can bring to bear, including virtual data rooms, due diligence tracking systems, document management, Gantt charts, etc.

Crucially, they have a keen ability to facilitate communication between all of the parties and keep everyone calm and on the same page.

CHAPTER 3

HOW MUCH WILL I GET FOR MY BUSINESS?

Valuing a business is part of our everyday job as we obviously need to come up with a price to go to market and then set the business Sellers' expectations as far as what they are likely to achieve. When selling businesses, the basic premise is that the business is really only worth what someone is willing to pay for it.

There are other reasons for valuing a business like divorce, partner buyouts, debt financing, etc. but we will focus on what a business might sell for and how the deal might be structured as generally that is what most business owners are curious about.

Business valuation can be one of the most misunderstood areas of the process in our experience. Business owners tend to have all kinds of ideas about what their business is worth when in fact the simple premise for most (non-asset-based) business sales is that a Buyer is buying the future cash flow discounted by a % which takes into account risk and expected ROI.

Unlike accounting which is mostly mathematical and rules based...business valuation tends to be 60% like accounting and 40% art or subjective. So there is a significant aspect that takes experience to navigate and a significant portion which is opinion based.

Further, business sale transactions are not a single number, they are generally a collection of commercial terms from the closing payment, deferred payments, loan notes, excess cash, rolled equity, earn-outs, etc These all need to be factored in and applied against risk factors.

And then there are the banks. Most businesses are bought with some debt (like buy-to-let flats) so Buyers are relying on some lending. The banks will often only lend up to a certain point and actually not lend on transactions they feel have been overvalued.

Lastly and almost most importantly; the cash flow has to work. The debt paid back to the bank, any deferred payments to the Seller, additional costs post-sale like a new Managing Director or Finance Director, etc. all have to be manageable within the available cash flow. Otherwise, the transaction does not work with that particular Buyer despite all the philosophical arguments around valuation.

Many times business Sellers will mention that their accountant, financial adviser, Uber driver, brother-in-law, etc. said their business was worth X. Upon further investigation there was no method used for this option and in fact none of these people is involved in daily working with buying and selling businesses in the real world. So the fact is there are methods and science that are helpful as at least as a foundation that gives us a starting point and a lens we can all work from.

An experienced business valuation/M&A professional can be very helpful to work through all the aspects of the valuation as well as work on the financial models (and negotiating) with any Buyers. But it is important the business owner understands the fundamentals to participate effectively in the process and make sure they feel they are getting the right (a good) deal in their own mind.

Components of a Business Sale Transaction

Businesses are rarely sold for a single 'number' like a car or a house. It is a package of components that are unique to the business and the specific Buyer.

Generally, these include:

Closing payment - Cash paid to Seller at closing.

Deferred payments - This is some sort of debt that is paid to the Seller over time, usually 2-4 years. The key point here is that it operates like debt and the Buyer has to pay it subject to warranties of course. These are a feature in the majority of business sales as they allow the business Seller to realise a higher value and also give the Buyer the comfort that the Seller is tied into the success of the business post-sale.

Excess Cash - Surplus to operations Cash/Working Capital can often be added to the sale price and closing payment. (see chapter on this subject)

Director Loan Write-Off - Often any directors loans on the balance sheet can be included in the business sale creating a Capital Gains Tax (generally 10% or 20%) effect instead of dividend tax which is normally declared to clear them at a year end if they are not going to be paid back.

Earn Out - These are payments based on milestones. We usually use them for revenue/profit that is over and above what the Seller is paying for based on normal business operations.

Sellers Post Sale Salary- Generally the Seller stays in the business for a period of time and is paid a salary for doing so.

Shares in the Buyer's Business - Sometimes the Buyer includes shares in their larger entity as part of the compensation for the sale. This is most common where the Seller is going to stay in the business for several years after the sale so wants a piece of the action.

Retention of Shares in the Seller's Business - Occasionally the Seller will retain a small shareholding in their own business as a minority shareholder.

Retention of Business Units in the Seller's Business - Occasionally the Seller will keep certain business units and sell the other to the Buyer. Think of an alarm company that also does fire systems servicing. The Seller might sell the alarm contracts but keep fire servicing.

Business Valuation Methods

There are basically three methods of valuation:

- Asset Method
- Income Method (Net Cash Flow)
- Market Method Using a Multiple

Asset Method

In general, for small/medium businesses (under £50M) are valued on their ability to produce profit/cash flow and therefore we would use one of the 2 methods below and not this method.

The asset method is generally used where the assets are not generating a profit that is greater than their value. So for example, a machine shop is running break even or at a loss and it is sometimes better just to sell the machines and inventory rather than trying to sell the going concern with goodwill. Sometimes this can be morphed into selling a customer list or recurring contracts but inevitably we revert to one of the methods below as the value is determined by the profitability.

It is important to note that you choose only one method and do not add them together...so if you use the Market Method below you do not add the fixed assets on top of it. The reason is that the assets are needed to produce profit. So, for example, you would buy a fish and chip shop for a certain ratio of the profit but you would expect the fish fryer, chairs, tables, refrigerators, etc that are used to run the shop to come with it and not suddenly be added as extras.

Income or Net Cash Flow (NCF) Method

This is probably the most accurate scientific way to value a business as you are taking the after tax, after everything cash flow that ends up back in the Buyers pocket and analysing that against a rate of return...very similar to how you would analyse a stock purchase on the public markets.

First, we have to determine what the cash flow into an investor's pocket will be each year. Although business valuation is all about the value to a Buyer in the future, normally we assume the business is going to run in a similar way as in the past. So we would generally take the last 3 years, maybe using some kind of weighting so that last year gets more emphasis than 3 years ago.

This cash flow would then be projected into the future and discounted back to a present value based on an expected rate of return. The rate of return calculation is complicated but in general, for small/medium businesses it ends up being mid-20s (i.e. 21% ish). This is similar to your home loan where the bank will give you £500K today for a cash flow of £2,000 per month for 30 years which is really £760K in total because of interest but the value today is £500K.

The good news for many people with glazed eyes at this point is that we don't tend to use this much in practice in the small/medium business arena as it is too difficult for all parties to get their heads around. But we like to explain it as it focuses the mind that the science part of the business valuation is a function of the business's ability to generate cash flow for the Buyer applied against an expected ROI/Risk factor.

Market Method Using a Multiple

The Market Method is the one that is generally used for profitable businesses when we work in the small/medium (under £50M) business arena. The basic premise is that we are comparing other, similar businesses that have sold based on some metric.

So a simple (but ludicrous just to make a point) one would be square footage. We could say that the last 10 fish and chips shops that were sold went for £500 per square foot of their shop. So if your shop is 300 square feet, we would say your shop would sell for £150K.

This is obviously much too crude so maybe we could next consider using revenue as the metric. The problem with revenue is that you can have one fish and chips shop on Oxford Street and one in the middle of nowhere, both doing £500K in revenue...which one is the most valuable? Well, the one on Oxford street is likely at a loss whereas the other one could be at a good profit due to drastically lower rents and staff costs so it would be more valuable as more after tax cash would flow back into the Buyer's pocket...so revenue does not work that well in most cases.

We could use operating profit before tax as a metric...the problem is that people put very different things through the company, many of which have nothing to do with the company. We notionally call these Ferraris and Hawaiian holidays as a tagline. Also, people do different things with salary and dividends as well as taxes so it is difficult to find commonality with just the Operating Profit figure on the annual report alone.

So the approach we take is to adjust this Operating Profit figure to calculate a number we call Adjusted EBITDA. EBITDA is earnings before Taxes, Interest, Depreciation and Amortisation.

The basic calculation is Adjusted EBITDA * a Multiple.

Adjusted EBITDA

For the Adjusted EBITDA calculation, we take the Operating Profit on the annual report and then 'add back' all the benefits that are going to the Seller. These can include the owner's salary (usually for 1 owner), director's pensions, director's cars and any other personal owner expenses. We also add back non-cash items like depreciation/amortisation and one-offs costs or loss of profit due to a fire or the company disposed of an asset. There also tend to be one-off adjustments for Covid impact and government grants related to the pandemic.

However, further complicating the equation is what time period do we measure Adjusted EBITDA for? The simple answer is that business valuation is based on the future cash flow so intrinsically we are trying to predict what future cash flow the Buyer will enjoy. However, historical financial performance is usually essential to determine what the future performance of the business will be.

What we generally do not do is just take the last 3 years and do an average. This would be saying that the performance 3 years ago was of equal value to determining performance as the previous year which for most SME businesses (especially those in growth) does not make sense.

With Covid, the results of many businesses in 2020/2021 have nothing to do with the future (some up/some down) so a view has to be taken. So there really is no correct answer for this that suits every situation and where the 'art' part of valuation comes in. The key is to keep the purpose of the exercise in mind which is to determine what next year is going to look like.

Multiples

A multiple is then applied against Adjusted EBITDA to come up with some idea of what to expect based on what others have sold for. But what multiple to use?

Many people throw out multiples as if they can be made up as some form of matter of opinion with no reference point. This is not true, we have many reference guides that do that analysis for us collating the data across 1000s of business sales so multiples are not just a finger in the air, there is real data behind it.

The next question is what drives these multiples. The simple answer is RISK.

A phenomenon of multiples is that as Adjusted EBITDA rises, risk decreases and multiples tend to go up. Think of an aeroplane in turbulence...the larger the plane, the less it is affected. This is why a company with £300K Adjusted EBITDA may have a 4x multiple and the exact same business with a £1.2M Adjusted EBITDA will attract a 6x multiple...there is less risk of one or two things happening that derail Adjusted EBITDA for example.

I have done 100s of pricing exercises and found that in general:

- Businesses on the High Street with under £200K Adjusted EBITDA sell for about a 1.5x - 2x multiple of Adjusted EBITDA
- Most businesses under £1M Adjusted EBITDA will attract a 3x or 4x multiple. Generally, if the business has recurring revenue and/or heavy equipment then this pushes the multiple up as risk is reduced.
- For a business that has Adjusted EBITDA over £1M, the multiples tend to go up to 5x/6x.
- As EBITDA rises up to £2m/£3M/£4M, etc the multiple go up again.

I have heard reports of brokers giving multiples far greater than these (sometimes triple!) but the data just doesn't back this up. Upon investigation, they are usually trying to persuade Sellers to pay a large upfront fee to sell their business and/or do not have the right education, experience and access to M&A data.

A trained M&A Advisor would of course need to do a comprehensive review of each business as they are all different but hopefully this gives you an idea. When a business sale process is initiated, part of the packaging process is to create a financial pack that outlines all of this for a potential Buyer to give everyone a good starting point. But it is only a starting point as in the end, it is about whether the Buyer and Seller want to do business and are willing to go through the process of putting a deal together that works for both parties.

CHAPTER 4

KEY FACTORS THAT AFFECT

VALUE

There are many factors that affect the value of a business...some subjective, some objective. One of the most important things to understand is that the main mathematical premise is that a Buyer is purchasing future cash flow so the level of confidence they have in the business's ability to produce that future cash flow will determine the level of risk they associate with the business which will, in turn, affect the valuation equation.

The Buyer will also assess how easy it will be for them to take over the business, how well it fits into their portfolio, cultural fit, geography relative to where they live or the location of their other businesses as well as whether they like the business or not at a personal level.

Main Areas a Buyer Will Look at That May Affect Value:

Good Books and Records – Demonstrates the company is well run and they can rely on the financial data being disclosed.

Quality of Revenue – What are the chances the revenue (and margins) will continue as it has historically? This is why recurring revenue, long-term contracts, long-term customers, etc. will cause the multiple to go up.

Size of Adjusted EBITDA – Mathematically valuation is often calculated as a multiple x Adjusted EBITDA therefore the higher the Adjusted EBITDA, the higher the valuation.

Key Man/Woman – The company needs to keep running and producing cash flow, people are most often key. If the owner leaves, does this create a risk for this cash flow? In an ideal situation, the owner will already have a management team and key people in place and the Buyer will assess there is little risk in a dip in operations.

Vendor Concentration and Dependency – If the company is heavily dependent on one or a few vendors this can be a red flag that increases risk. What happens if they decide to stop supplying? What about other contractual relationships that could suddenly disrupt business operations?

Documented Processes – Having documented processes versus a few people in the middle of everything to keep things going increases the confidence the Buyer has that the transition post-sale will be smooth. An operations manual that documents these processes is ideal. Also, most often Buyers know companies that are process based and well documented are easier to scale and grow.

The Above Aspects are Covered in More Detail Below:

Good Books and Records are Key to Selling a Business

During our training as business advisers and in all of our material we are told the three most important things to have ready when selling a business are:

- Good Books and Records
- Good Books and Records
- Good Books and Records

This is similar to the location, location, location mantra when selling real estate. Of course, it does not tell the whole story but the very experienced people who come up with this are just trying to make an important point that can not be overlooked in almost every circumstance.

One of the big reasons good books and records are so important is that businesses are generally valued based on their ability to generate cash flow for the Buyer in the future (see previous blogs for more details on this).

We have previously said that business sales are 60% heart and 40% head for the Buyer...but the head stuff matters. This is similar to buying a house...you and your partner need to love the house but then the finances have to work, the kid's schools have to be close enough, work needs to be a decent travel distance, etc. You will never be able to buy the house if the payments are double your salary and the commute to work is 3 hours each way for example.

In a similar way, the Buyer needs to know that the cash flow produced by the business is going to be able to pay for any debt service, deferred payments to the Seller, enough for risk mitigation and still have enough left over for the Buyer to make a living if he needs to or enough of a return if he is an absentee Buyer.

I am always amazed at how some Sellers gloss over this point and think the Buyer will 'get' their business and think that the excuse of not being 'very into accounts' will somehow make poor or old books and records ok with the Buyer.

I can tell you from experience, it does not. If the Buyer does like the business and we proceed with due diligence, all that happens is that we get down towards the end and due diligence fails as the Buyer realises they cannot prove the cash flow...and we generally all conclude we have wasted several months and the Buyer should come back in 12 months while the Seller cleans up his books and records.

So what do we mean by good books and records? The following are the things we need for a good financial pack. They need to be accurate and up to date and provable in due diligence:

1. Filed accounts for the last 3 fiscal years (the un-abbreviated version of what is filed at Companies House) - this should be easy as the accountant produces these for every fiscal year end by law.

2. Management Accounts (Profit and Loss and Balance Sheet) through last month since the last year end (i.e. since the last filed accounts date) - These normally come out of the accounting system (i.e. Sage, Xero, QuickBooks). We do not expect the balance sheets to be accurate as the accountant will not have done any adjustments but we can compensate for that when we do the recast for the financial pack.

3. Aged debtors and aged creditors (2 different reports) as of the last month - This comes out of your accounting system. Sometimes we need to wait for your bookkeeper to catch up with the last month end which is fine...we will wait.

4. Asset list over £5000 - This is a list of assets in the business with their market values (Seller estimate). This is not the book value with depreciation schedules although these will be needed in DD. This is to ascertain the value of the assets in the business for valuation and for obtaining commercial lending.

5. Bank statements for the last 3 months - Self-explanatory and should just come right out of the online banking system.

6. VAT statements for the last 4 quarters - this will be available at the HMRC VAT portal.

There are a few notes to make on the above:

Businesses that have a lot of undeclared cash - (you know who you are ;-) They will need special handling. We can help with that on a case-by-case basis. In general, we give the Buyer the idea of the cash you are taking and then he will need to prove this in due diligence, there are many methods for this.

However, we advise people to stop taking cash when they enter into a business sale process as we are generally getting 2x or 3x for every £1 a profit whereas you are only saving .19x in corporation tax when you don't declare the cash. Even after a few months of everything going through the books, it may be enough to convince a Buyer of your real sales and get you 100% value for your real profit.

Businesses that work on a % completion method (i.e. builders) - These require the accountant to calculate the revenues, costs and WIP based on the progress of projects. Usually, they will do this twice a year so we may have to use previous financials and then look at cash flow, new contracts, etc. to ascertain the business is still performing at the same level. These businesses should have no problem producing the above reports but the profit (EBITDA) figures will need to be calculated by the accountant and we will come up with strategies during due diligence to work with this.

Businesses that take a lot of pre-payments spanning many months/ years - Typically we find the revenue and profit are recognised in a very conservative fashion to minimise tax. As with the above point, the accountant typically needs to come in and adjust the financials in order to reflect revenue and profits correctly. These are generally great businesses with recurring revenue so worth the effort but it is not as simple as producing an accounting system report.

Quality of Earnings

Valuation is mathematically based on EBITDA which in turn is driven by sales and gross profit. During the due diligence process, the Buyer will be determining what they think the ongoing EBITDA is going to be post-sale. This will drive the valuation, lending, cash flow, etc. Gaining confidence in this revenue stream is therefore critical.

The Buyer will almost certainly assess the strength and predictability of the client base during due diligence. Generally, they will become uncomfortable if one customer has more than 15% of the revenue as this creates a big hole if this customer were to suddenly stop trading with the company for example.

The Buyer will also be looking at debt collection. Customers that are not paying on time, especially over 90 days represent a risk that they may never pay at all or not pay the next invoices due to financial issues.

Long-term contracts are ideal but repeating customers who have been buying for a long time are also very good. Sometimes contracts create 'cliffs' where the customer will need to re-evaluate whereas a long-term repeat customer who is habituated to buying from the company could go on for years with no review...so it just depends.

The overall objective is to assess the likelihood that the sales volume will continue to drive the profit that the transaction is based on. Often if there is a concern about specific customers some of the valuations can be based on future collections as an earn-out and/or warranties can be introduced if customers were to disappear within an agreed time period.

Size of Adjusted EBITDA

There is no getting away from the fact that Adjusted EBITDA drives valuation in most transactions therefore it makes sense that we want this to be as large as possible. It is important to remember that we are interested in future cash flow so we have to be able to prove to the Buyer that this will continue after they own the company post-sale.

The most basic ways to increase EBITDA are to increase sales/turnover (at the same margins), increase margins on existing sales or reduce administrative/operating expenses. Often investments have to be made to increase sales in one year that will manifest in the next year like hiring additional salespeople or buying additional capital equipment so this needs to be taken into account and balanced with how quickly the Seller wants to sell the business.

For Sellers that have a few years before selling, we suggest working with a business optimisation consultant to come up with strategies around this.

Key Man/Woman

The Buyer will normally be looking for the business to run smoothly after the Seller leaves. As always, the Buyer wants to make sure that the business keeps running and the profit is not impacted. Due to this, there will normally need to be someone or a few people that can step up at least operationally. Often the Buyer will run a non-exec board that will take care of strategic planning but will be relying on the key people to run the business day to day.

For this reason, it is important that these people are identified, operating as leaders when the Buyer starts looking at the business and that the Seller has backed away from the business as much as possible. We always say we like it when Sellers talk about how much golf they play or how many holidays they go on. This gives the Buyer confidence that the business can run without them.

The lack of a key person (s) is one of the main reasons a financial Buyer (i.e Private Equity) will reject a company for consideration. It is like having a plane with no pilot. It is generally very difficult to hire people from the outside into this position so this is generally not a viable short-term solution.

Documented Process

Many companies have few documented processes and rely heavily on a few individuals being involved to keep everything running. This is even more exacerbated when one of these individuals is the Seller. The problem with this is that if one of these people is removed for some reason, the business can suffer. This type of model is also not very scalable as it bottlenecks these individuals. This creates risk (and hassle) for the Buyer post-sale which will often knock onto a business's valuation.

The solution to this is to move to a more process-oriented approach. One way to address this is to create an operations manual which documents all of the processes in the business. This exercise will force a re-evaluation and documentation of these processes often leading to natural efficiency improvements. The operations manual will also give the Buyer great comfort that the business can be understood and scaled beyond certain people. Also, in some cases, the operations manual can be used to 'franchise' the business to other locations.

This is a somewhat specialised area and we would normally suggest engaging a business consultant who can assist with this process.

Vendor Concentration and Dependency

Some businesses are dependent on one or two vendors for the majority of what they make or sell. Should one of these relationships suddenly decide not to do business with them it could have a detrimental impact on the company and cash flow. So the Buyer will want to assess this risk as well as the viability of replacement.

This can also arise in licensing situations like a franchise where the franchisor would cut off certain territories or products on short notice or even refuse to approve the sale full stop.

Risk can also arise where most of the revenue is from one or two suppliers who will continue to supply but there is a risk the product lines they supply will no longer be in demand in the future (i.e. fall out of fashion). In these cases, the ability and method to add new product lines must be assessed. Often this is a task done by the Seller historically so the Buyer needs to assess if they can learn the skills and build the contract networks necessary to keep a flow of new products being added.

CHAPTER 5

DEAL STRUCTURES

Selling a Business Via an Asset Sale Versus a Share Sale

There are basically two ways to execute a business transaction which are to sell the assets in the business or sell the shares in a Limited Company company. There are some variations on this with LLPs and other vehicles, but I will stick to asset sales and the sale of the shares in a Limited Company for this chapter as they represent 98% of the transactions we work on..

Asset Sale

Description - This is as it sounds, the assets in the business are sold as a collective or individually to a Buyer/Buyers Limited Company.. If the business is profitable, then a premium may be added to the value of the assets and specified as 'goodwill'. As discussed previously, businesses are normally sold for the ability to generate cash flow. The assets in the business enable this cash flow to be realised so there is a value for the assets themselves and a further value for their ability to generate cash flow, the difference being goodwill.

If the business is not profitable, the assets are usually just being sold at market value and often not as a collective as the business may not survive in its current form (what is the point if it is loss-making?) Assets sales are normally transacted with an Asset Purchase Agreement (APA). This will have schedules denoting which assets are being sold as well as the release of liability and other legal aspects that the solicitor will add.

What is Included - Generally the physical assets that are needed for the business to operate like machinery, cooking equipment, tables/chairs, etc. Also, any intangible property like websites, brand names, patents, etc. Pretty much everything that is needed to run the business to continue to generate the cash flow that is being purchased. The lease is also generally included in the sale and may attract a premium over the face value. This is subject to the landlord approving the transfer of course.

What is Not Included - Generally an asset sale is cash free/debt free. So cash, the debtor's book (almost cash) and any liabilities are retained by the Seller. This can be negotiated, but this is usually the starting point. The contracts with customers and suppliers for these generally are with the Seller or the Sellers company and do not transfer automatically.

What About Stock - Stock is an anomaly as it is constantly changing and is needed to run the business. There are also issues with counting it, what is actually sellable, what its true value, etc. Most business sales are done with a purchase price for the assets plus stock at value (SAV) on closing day. This is an area that is subject to negotiation on a case-by-case basis.

What Happens to Existing Contractual Relationships - As the Buyer is just buying the assets, they have to sign their own contracts for everything related to their new business including leases, employees, utilities, etc. There are mechanisms in place to make the transfer of these fairly straightforward in most cases but the people and companies will be contracting with a new legal entity (i.e. the Buyer as an individual or their new Limited Company that bought the assets).

How Are the Assets Versus Goodwill Valued - This is sometimes a big point of contention as the Seller wants the value of the assets to be as low as possible to avoid any capital gains tax and the Buyer wants it as high as possible to be able to depreciate the assets and offset taxes. Normally, the assets are valued at the market value at the time and the difference in the sale price is attributed to goodwill, but this is subject to negotiation.

Share Sales

Description - In this case, a Buyer is buying the shares of the Limited Company (UK) and therefore everything contained within. The Buyers name will be denoted as the new owner of the shares at Companies House and they will be listed as a director. This means the company will retain all of its existing relationships, contracts, and liabilities (including HMRC) just as before.

Share sales are normally transacted with a Share Purchase Agreement (SPA). A SPA is far more complicated than an Asset Purchase Agreement as the Buyer is taking every aspect of the business including the liabilities so great care has to be taken. Warranties and Indemnities for any liabilities that crop up post-sale are normally part of the SPA and can be offset against any future payments.

What is Included - Everything that is owned, contracted or owed by the Limited Company is included unless certain assets are specifically excluded. This includes all the assets and liabilities on the balance sheet, customers, employees, intangible assets, etc.

As this includes all of the liabilities and contractual obligations of the Limited Company, significant due diligence has to be undertaken to make sure the Buyer understands what they are liable for. Also, warranties are typically introduced in case liabilities arise in the future or assets which are integral to the sale do not perform (i.e. customers leave).

What is Not Included - Often there is excess cash in the business which can be returned to the owner. The amount of this is subject to negotiation. Also, long-term loans and directors' loans are generally settled at closing and do not transfer with the business, but this is also subject to negotiation as there is sometimes benefit in leaving them on the balance sheet.

There may also be historical contingencies like an outstanding court case where the Seller will be liable depending on the outcome in the future. Typically, there are deferred payments to the Seller that can be adjusted for these items.

What About Stock and Existing Contractual Relationships - The Limited Company keeps running as normal, only the ownership changes. So unless there is negotiation otherwise, everything in the Limited Company stays in place and there is just status quo the day after closing but under new ownership.

How Are the Assets Versus Goodwill Valued - The Seller's accountant will need to calculate a capital gain for tax purposes. The Buyer can choose to add goodwill to the balance sheet based on consultation with their accountant.

Advantages/Disadvantages of a Share Sale versus an Asset Sale

The advantage of an asset sale is that it is simple as the Seller is responsible for all of the previous liabilities and retains the cash assets in the business. The problem with an asset sale is that the Buyer has to create new contractual relationships with the bank, employees, suppliers, customers, franchisor, etc.

For some businesses, these relationships are multi-faceted and cannot be reestablished in the short run. In this case, a share sale is far more efficient as all of the contractual relationships stay intact (including the bank) and the business continues to operate as normal.

The disadvantage of a share sale is that it is much more complicated contractually as the Buyer, as a director, is now going to be responsible for managing all the liabilities of the business. Warranties can be put in place to cover anything unexpected but much more due diligence is necessary and a much more thorough contractual framework.

Just to mention that the vast majority of the business sales we do over £1M Enterprise Value are Share Sales in the United Kingdom. We understand from our US colleagues that Asset Sales are most common there. This has to do with many factors including different tax and lending regimes.

Financing a Business Sale

When selling a business, it is not common for a Buyer to have 100% of the proceeds in cash to be paid upfront for many reasons. Hence many forms of financing are often needed to put transactions together.

Commercial Loans

Most businesses are bought with some kind of debt or leverage. The easy comparison is how most property investments are also bought with debt (i.e. buy to let flats). In the case of a property investment, rarely would someone with £1M buy 1 x £1M flat, they would buy 4x £1M flats with £250K each down and finance the rest with the payments to the bank being made from the profit from the rentals.

Most of the time Buyers will work with specialist finance agents who in turn work with specialist lenders who specialise in Mergers and Acquisition lending in its various forms. Occasionally, Buyers will use High Street banks as the rates tend to be lower but these can be very difficult and time-consuming.

Commercial loans are generally taken out and the proceeds are given to the Buyer at closing as part of the closing payment. The reason this is not 100% of the sale value is that in very few situations will the banks lend this amount, the difference often being made up by deferred payments or Sellers notes (see below).

Asset-Backed Loans Based on Debtors' Books - These are generally taken with the debtor book as the guarantee, with some small portion for fixed assets. This can be between 50-90% of the value of the debtor book for example. They generally operate like revolving credit meaning only the interest needs to be paid and the loan rates are reasonable so they often do not put the business under a lot of stress.

Asset Backed Loans Based on Fixed Assets - These are loans which are guaranteed against machines, vehicles, property or any other fixed asset on the balance sheet. They tend to be over around 5 years and principal and interest are due on a monthly basis so cash flow is more impacted than debtor book loans.

Also, the amount banks will lend against assets is usually only a fraction of what the market value may be so these form generally the smallest part of the debt package in most transactions.

Cash Flow Term Loans - These are based on the viability of the business and generally paid over something like a 5-year term at 10%+ interest. As the interest and principal are payable, there needs to be sufficient cash flow in the business to sustain these.

Also, as the payments are often significant, if the business runs into trouble it can be difficult to negotiate with the lender which could put the business in jeopardy. Generally, they will loan up to a maximum of 2.5x of EBITDA but the payments have to be affordable by the business, which often means the loan value is less. Generally, the banks will want the Buyer to put 10-15% of their own (hurt) money into the transaction. They will also have capital ratios that need to be maintained.

Government Backed Loans - These are products that reduce the banks' risk as the government will guarantee all or most of the loans. These tend to have limits but can be easier for Buyers to take out. These loans tend to be over 5-6 years and payment of interest and principal is monthly so the cash flow impact must be planned very carefully.

Deferred Payments

On the day a business sale transaction takes place, the Seller is given an amount of cash called a 'closing payment'. Most often there is a difference between the closing payment and the sale price which must be bridged. Very often a deal is struck where the balance is paid over a period of time, generally 2-5 years on a monthly, quarterly or annual basis. Because the valuation is based on future cash flow, it makes sense at one level that the Seller receives the benefit as the cash flow when it is realised.

Deferred payments are a very common feature in small business sales. At first glance, a Seller may not want to entertain such an instrument. However, upon examination, they realise that they are often necessary in order to get the full value out of the business.

The basic reason for this is that a Buyer may only have so much money they can put into the transaction and the bank debt that can be taken for the sale is limited so the difference has to be made up with a deferred payment if the Seller wants to sell to that Buyer.

It is important to understand that deferred payments are an actual debt owed to the Seller and are generally not contingent. They are a form of Seller financing where the Seller is basically replacing the bank. Sometimes there will be an interest rate associated with this amount and sometimes it is just straight division based on the number of periods of the deferred payment.

Another aspect to be aware of is that deferred payments are paid out of the profits of the company. This is important as the business needs to be able to afford them. There is no point in making deferred payments higher than the business can afford only to have the business run out of money and no longer be able to operate and therefore not able to make the rest of the deferred payments!

The next question that always arises is how secure are the deferred payments?

Deferred payments are debt and function like debt. Very often the Seller will insist on a fixed and floating charge over the assets of the business and a charge at Companies House. Another common Seller demand is to implement 'capital controls' so no assets can be removed from the business, expensive staff cannot be hired, significant assets purchased, etc. until the deferred payments are settled. So the only risk of not getting paid is if the company goes out of business in which case the Buyer will also lose their money.

We have heard many stories of people losing out on deferred payments when they sell their business. When we investigate further, it is usually because the business sale contracts were not written well with the appropriate controls in place.

We have also heard of people getting burgled frequently who refuse to put alarms, appropriate locks and camera systems on their facilities. The reality in practice is that, with the help of lawyers and advisors, many controls can be put in place that protects the Seller as long as the business is still viable.

Deferred Payments are commonly paid quarterly. As yearly is too long and too much can change and monthly can be an administrative burden.

Sometimes a Buyer will insist on warranties that mitigate some of the risks of deferred payments. As the Buyer is buying future cash flow, there can be some kind of warranty that the business they have bought will perform as expected. This takes many forms depending on the business.

Common warranties are around customer retention, employees staying in place, expected cash flows from contracts continuing, etc. The idea is that the cash flow is what the Buyer is buying and if it does not happen, the Seller should take some of the risk. If half the customers leave after 6 months and the cash flow is impacted, for example, there is a warranty issue.

Variable Payments/Earn Outs

This is any type of post-sale payment that has a contingency on performance tied to it. There are several terms for this including earn-out which does not mean the Seller has to stay in the business and 'earn' something. It simply means that the additional payments are earned through some kind of pre-agreed mechanism that generally means the business is performing better than expected.

The most common reason the need for this arises is when the Seller feels the business is going to do better than the historical Adjusted EBITDA would demonstrate. Generally, they will feel that contracts are closing or revenue is coming in that was put in place by them but will have a benefit to the Buyer after the sale date.

It is also common to use earn-outs when the business is experiencing high growth. The Buyer only wants to value future cash flow based on historical financial statements but the Seller believes future cash flows will be materially different due to the growth curve.

One of the most common types of earn-outs is for the Buyer and Seller to share excess Adjusted EBITDA. This makes sense as the Adjusted EBITDA is the basis of the valuation and cash flow. This can take many forms but often scales down over time (i.e. 2-3 years) with the idea that the Buyer is actually driving the growth as time goes on.

However, monitoring Adjusted EBITDA can be very tricky in practice. Once the broad line numbers are agreed upon, it is common to go up the P&L and use gross profit or even revenue/sales as a driving metric. This can be derived based on a formula or other means but it is much easier to measure and monitor.

Seller Notes

Seller notes are similar to deferred payments in that they bridge the difference between the closing payment and the business value.

However, the difference usually is that the Seller Note only pays interest or a coupon payment each year until expiry when they are paid in full. They are generally secured against the business as junior debt.

Many Sellers like Seller notes as they can attract quite a high-interest rate (i.e. 8% - 12%) so could consider some of their proceeds ' pre-invested' so to speak. Buyers like Seller notes as they can pay the interest only out of profits and the budget or refinance to cover the expiry payout.

Occasionally the Seller may want to replace the role of the commercial lender in full. What can happen is that the Seller realises that they will be receiving a windfall at closing but may not have any good investment opportunities.

They may further realise that an 8% - 12% return is far better than they will get from most other investments with reasonable risk. They may determine it makes more sense for them to take on the cash flow/term loan themselves and get the interest. This may be deemed a less risky investment in something they understand and can control.

Usually, this gives the Seller the position of senior debt with all the collection rights that entails. They can also demand regular reports, review meetings and control mechanisms they can execute if they feel the business is in trouble. In short, they have the right to ask for visibility and control until the debt is paid. This is something they are unlikely to get on other investments and so is appealing to many Sellers.

CHAPTER 6

WORKING CAPITAL AND EXCESS CASH

This discussion is only generally necessary for a share sale where all the elements of the working entity are being purchased inside a Limited Company container so to speak. In an Asset Sale, generally many of these elements are not included especially cash and debt so the following is only relevant for a Share Sale.

Determining the right level of working capital and excess cash distributions to the Seller is a critical step in the business sale process. This discussion can often be robust as it has a direct $$/££ impact on both parties at closing. The Buyer wants to make sure the risk of running out of money is low, the Seller wants as much as possible as what they will often view as their money!

The challenge is that the calculations are often highly technical on one hand and driven by the accountants. On the other hand, the final formula is a matter of judgment on which the Buyer and Seller must come to an agreement. Our advice is just to realize this is a challenging discussion, work through it methodically with the right advice and professionals and realize there will be some give and take that does not really include anyone winning or losing but just different lenses.

Terminology

Cash Free/Debt Free

Most businesses are sold on a debt-free/cash-free basis. What this means in practice is that the long-term debts including accrued taxation are covered by the Seller either out of their existing cash or closing payment. This also means that any excess cash is returned to the Seller as this usually represents profit that has not been extracted yet. However, usually, there is the expectation that a reasonable or minimal amount of working capital (and cash) is left in the business so it can operate under normal conditions.

Excess Cash

Excess working capital generally manifests as excess cash in the business so this is what most people relate to as it seems intuitive to watch a bank balance grow to more than is required for the business to operate. However, it is necessary to factor in all the requirements for cash in a business, especially outstanding and/or upcoming debts like bank loans and taxes in order to get an accurate picture. For this reason, a proper analysis of 'working capital' is necessary. This also needs to take into account seasonality and other time-related aspects of the business cycle.

Excess Working Capital

Generally, excess working capital exists in a business as profits have been accumulated that have not been reinvested, paid off debt or taken out as a dividend. These accumulated profits are considered excess to operations (not needed for the business to produce the cash flow) and could be removed via dividend prior to a sale without impacting the viability of the business (although this may not be the best method from a tax perspective as below).

This means the fixed and net current assets (i.e. debtors, stock, creditors, etc. and a minimum amount of cash) on the balance sheet are what is transferred. Just specifying 'cash free/debt free' is generally too simplistic as it does not take into account things like debtors/stock turns and when creditors are due that could require cash in the bank.

For example, what would happen if the Seller got all the customers to pay early so that on closing day there were no debtors and just cash in the bank which the Seller would sweep out? The Buyer would be left with creditors but no customer receipts to cover them. Hence the analysis of working capital compressively is more reflective of the nuances of cash flow. This is covered in more detail below.

Tax Considerations

Once an estimate of the Excess Working Capital is calculated it is technically possible for the Seller to extract this from the business prior to the sale as a dividend without harming the operations of the business. However, this will generally cause a tax event for the Seller with many paying 40%+ in tax on this extraction.

Often a more tax-efficient method is to add the excess working capital to the business sale value. This means the Seller is then only taxed at Capital Gains tax rates (usually 10% under £1M and 20% over £1m per person currently in the UK). The effect is that of the Buyer 'buying the excess cash from the Seller'. (Note: This is just meant to be for discussion, each Buyer/Seller should check their individual situation with their tax advisor).

Long Term Debts

Generally, long-term debts need to be paid off prior to closing as they were part of the means the Seller used to finance the business. These include things like Bounce Back loans, Funding Circle, bank loans, etc. Often what looks like excess working capital is simply these loans that are still in the bank account so to speak and need to be paid back. If there is not sufficient cash in the business to satisfy these loans, usually the

Seller's closing payment is reduced and the Buyer takes on or pays these loans with those funds.

Director's Loan Accounts (DLA)

A business sale can often be an opportunity to have DLAs cleared and only incur capital gains tax (CGT on business sales is 10% or 20% at the time of this writing). DLAs are money disbursed or payments made to the directors that are not payroll and are operational to the business (i.e. such as business expense reimbursement). Typically, the DLA account is used as a sort of placeholder for shareholder disbursements and is turned into dividends by the accountant when the year-end accounts are done. DLA's must be paid back within 9 months of the fiscal year-end or a tax must be paid by the company (32.5% at the time of this writing). When a business sale transaction happens, the Seller can declare a dividend prior to the business sale to clear the DLA but this can often attract 40%+ tax depending on the amount. Alternatively, the DLA can be paid back on the day of sale from the proceeds of the closing payment. This, in turn, becomes excess cash which is returned to the Seller on closing day and in effect increases the sale value hence attracting only the capital gains tax amount. As always, advice should be taken from an appropriate tax advisor as there are nuances.

Calculating Working Capital (Net Current Assets)

Working capital is the current assets and liabilities of a business that continuity goes up and down as the business continues to operate. The elements of working capital are like a piston that goes round and round with one side high and another lower only to switch back but always maintaining a balance and momentum.

The common elements of working capital on the balance sheet are below:

Current Assets

- Cash

- Debtors - customers who owe the business
- Stock
- Work in Progress
- Pre-Payments – Money the business has paid in advance

Current Liabilities

- Creditors – suppliers to who the business owes
- Payroll taxes owed as of now
- VAT owed as of now
- Accruals – Money the business owes but creditors have not invoiced
- Corporation tax owed as of now
- Customer deposits
- Other cash and short-term debt items

Note: We normally exclude the Director's Loans and Inter Company Loan accounts for the working capital calculation as the assumption is Director's Loans will just be turned into a dividend or written off at closing and Interco Loans are written off so have no impact on cash flow.

An example of a working capital calculation for Best Body Whole Foods would be:

- Cash - £350K
- Stock - £150K
- Debtors - £400K
- Trade Creditors - (£350K)
- VAT (£150K)
- Payroll Taxes (£10K)
- Corp Tax Accrual (£90K)

Net Working Capital = £300K

Minimum Working Capital (Working Capital PEG/Normalised Working Capital)

These terms are generally used to mean the same thing. When all the working capital elements above are aggregated (added up), this number is what we call net working capital. If the net working capital becomes too low, the business feels like it is under pressure normally manifested as not having enough money to pay creditors or payroll when they are due. At some point, this will need to be rectified by injecting more cash (working capital) into the business via a loan or capital from the shareholders.

A business Buyer expects to purchase a working business that will not need more cash injected later so it is important to determine a minimum working capital to avoid this. One of these three terms is generally used to denote what this number is.

There are several methods for determining what a minimum working capital figure should be although there can be many nuances depending on the business:

Average Working Capital Over a Twelve-Month Period

In this method, the average working capital over a 12-month (or agreed) period is examined and the average is set as the minimum working capital figure. The challenge in this method is to determine how much was excess during the 12-month period...often cash is excluded or minimised for this calculation for that reason.

One caveat is that if the business is in growth, it will require more working capital so the prior year will not be indicative of the current run rate and/or need to be adjusted. Also, seasonality will need to be taken into account so the business does not run low on working capital during quiet months.

Net Current Assets at Zero

In this method it is assumed that the business is cash generative so having current assets and liabilities balanced to zero will result in a situation where the business will not run out of cash. This often works well as the current assets in the form of debtors are often collected faster than many of the current liabilities need to be paid, especially items like Corp tax so the business is always ahead so to speak.

This can work well for some businesses but fall over for others that have very slow payment terms from customers or long lead times from stock purchase to a stock sale. This also can become unworkable if growth is steep which requires more working capital to keep up.

Cash Flow Modelling

In this method, a cash flow projection is constructed over at least the next 12 months but generally longer. This will allow a clear view of what excess working capital manifesting in cash is over a longer period and allow a clear view of what cash could be taken out a closing without causing the cash balance to go dangerously low in the future.

This is often the method easiest for both Buyer and Seller to understand but requires a focused project working with both sets of accountants. One caveat of this method is that the Seller is selling the business as it is running today...if the Buyer wants to grow it this is great, but it is not up to the Seller to provide working capital for them to do so.

Others

The objective of determining a minimum working capital level is that the business does not run out of money at some point in the future based on the current operating level. Often there are many technical nuances that require the Buyer and Seller's accountants to come to a joint conclusion using a hybrid of these methods.

Methods for Managing Working Capital During a Business Sale Process

Closing Accounts Method

With this method, a target working capital figure is specified either at the Heads of Terms/LOI stage or at some stage during the Due Diligence phase. Again, getting the parties to agree on this can be contentious so the assistance of a qualified M&A Advisor can be helpful in managing the discussion. It is unlikely that both sides' accountants will agree on this figure and there are likely to be philosophical differences on what constitutes working capital. However, at some point, a figure that the Seller is committing to the Buyer will be on the balance sheet on closing day and must be agreed upon.

Once this figure is agreed upon and the business sale closes on a particular day (month ends are easiest), the accountants will need a period of time (i.e. a month or two) to determine exactly what the balance sheet was on closing day which we call preparing closing accounts. The working capital figure on this balance sheet is compared to the target working capital figure and any overages are paid back to the Seller and any underages are generally deducted either from any closing payment retention or the Seller's next deferred payment.

This method is often used when the transaction is simple and the professional accountants and advisors' time on a transaction is minimal. This is because there are just two points where analysis needs to happen around the working capital figure and then the preparation of the closing accounts. These can easily be done by the incumbent accountant as discrete projects.

Lock Box Method

With this method an offer on the business is made based on a specific balance sheet, usually, the last year-end filed accounts. This then becomes the 'effective date' with the purchaser taking on the risk of the business's performance from that date.

The Seller is then contractually obligated not to take resources out of the business (i.e. cash, dividends, equipment) beyond the 'leakage' that has been agreed with the Buyer. They are also under constraints to run the businesses normally on a day-to-day basis and not make any major capital expenditures, commitments for staff, inventory changes, etc. without the consent of the Buyer.

If the period between agreeing on the offer and closing is lengthy, the Seller will want the benefit of the profit generated during that period and can agree to adjustments at closing often called 'stub' payments.

The advantage is that it eliminates the uncertainty and post-sale efforts involved in producing closing accounts. The disadvantage is that the Seller is constrained in running their business and if the transaction does not close they could lose momentum during that period when they may have made other investment decisions, etc. It can also become very complex to manage over the due diligence period to ensure there are no anomalies so generally this requires more advisor time and focus.

CHAPTER 7

TYPES OF BUYERS

There are many different types of Buyers but they can broadly be discussed in three categories which are **Investor/Financial Buyers, Trade/Strategic Buyers, Operator Buyers, Management Buy Outs (MBO) and Employee Ownership Trusts (EOT).**

Trade or Strategic Buyers

Trade or strategic Buyers are trading companies that are often looking at doing acquisitions as a growth strategy. They are often larger versions of the Sellers' company or in the same sector. This is not necessarily the case as a company may be looking to add a business unit in an area they have not been involved in, a new geography or acquire technology or staff.

Advantages

One of the big advantages of Trade or Strategic Buyers is that they may be in the same sector as the Seller so will have a good understanding of how the Seller business operates. This can make a sale process much more straightforward as they may know exactly what they are looking for and how to fill any gaps. Their understanding of the business will also reduce risk relative to another type of Buyer and with reduced risk goes upward pressure on valuation.

They may also be able to cross-pollinate management teams which may lessen the impact of the Seller owner leaving the business.

This type of Buyer may be able to gain efficiencies by reducing overheads, cross-selling products and using tax efficiencies. These can increase cash flow allowing for better deal structures and faster payment terms.

This type of Buyer may instantly gain an uplift in valuation multiples with an acquisition creating an added motivation and financial scope for doing the transaction.

Disadvantages

Often the Seller has key people that will be ready to run the business once they leave and in fact have been waiting for this opportunity. A trade Buyer who is already in the business sector may not offer them this opportunity and they may find themselves absorbed into a management structure where they are more junior or completely eliminated. While the business Seller may profit from this type of transaction financially, they may not want a scenario where their loyal lieutenants who are ready to be promoted are disadvantaged.

Often a Trade Buyer who is in the same sector will think they know better how to run the Seller's business (we use the analogy of Gordon Ramsey never liking a kitchen he walks into!). This can be uncomfortable for a Seller who is proud of their legacy and wants to see the business and people continue on their current trajectory.

These types of Buyers run their own businesses as their main focus and often do not have extensive experience in Mergers and acquisitions (in contrast to a financial Buyer who does acquisitions as a business focus).

Following the above point, many of these types of Buyers have deployed their capital running their businesses and are not well funded for business acquisitions. However, this is not always the case as many have been very profitable and are looking to use these profits for acquisitions so with Trade Buyers it is very much case by case.

Investor or Financial Buyers

Investors or Financial Buyers are Buyers that invest, grow and sell companies as their business model. These come in two general categories – Private Equity and private investment groups or individual investors.

Private Equity (PE) Buyers

This type of Buyer is FCA-regulated company that raises capital from investors, buys companies, grow companies and sell them for a profit. Usually, they will achieve around a 3x increase in value over a 3-7 year period. Currently, there is over £1T of uninvested PE funds in the world today.

The reason is that the returns on this model make this one of the best investment vehicles available. However, due to the effort involved in doing an acquisition, PE firms in the UK will typically start looking at companies with over £1M EBITDA with a preference over £1.5M EBITDA.

Private Investment Groups or Individual Investors

This type of Buyer runs a similar model in that they buy companies, grow them and sell them for a profit. The difference is that they tend to use their own money or people close to them and leverage debt to fund the acquisitions. Due to this, they tend to buy the companies that are smaller than the PE firms (i.e. below £1M EBITDA) but the model they are running is similar.

Advantages

Investor/Financial Buyers buy companies as part of their business model so the successful ones have a high level of competency and understand the process. This means that there is a much greater chance of completing a transaction and the process will run smoother.

This type of Buyer is also generally totally dependent on the existing management team which is ideal for the Seller owner's second tier that wants to step up and run the business. In that case, the transaction can almost function like an MBO where these individuals are promoted and given sweet equity (free equity given by the Buyer) to hit targets and grow the business so it is very good for them.

This Buyer type will probably have bought many companies and developed experience in how to grow different kinds of companies after acquisition. They will usually put a 5-year plan in place, a non-exec board that meets once a month and includes the Seller's key second-tier person as well as a grey-haired chairman. Often they will introduce a Finance Director or sales and marketing acceleration. All things that they have learned contribute to the business being able to leverage the current model to achieve significant growth.

Disadvantages

Investor/Financial Buyers don't usually run companies so if the Seller has a weak second tier, this can be an issue. Also, they may need to bring in outside people to compensate for the loss of skills when the owner leaves, further complicating the transaction. If there is a cost for these people (i.e. like a Finance Director) this will reduce the Adjusted EBITDA from their perspective and possibly the valuation.

PE firms are very well funded but they buy relatively few businesses. This means a Seller below the £1M Adjusted EBITDA threshold may be engaging with investment groups or individual investors who often are not that well funded. This can be overcome to some degree with debt but it can put cash flow pressure on the transaction.

Operator Buyers

An Operator Buyer is someone who is buying the business to run it themselves. They may or may not have experience in the businesses they are buying. If they don't have experience, the handover period may be much longer as the Seller will need to train them. Often this is not just one person but maybe a husband/wife team or two or more people that are looking to do a project together. This type of sale is normally good for smaller, owner-operated businesses that do not have a second-tier management structure.

Advantages

One of the big advantages is that the Seller is going to run the business so the sale is not so dependent on the key person to run the business post-sale. This kind of Buyer will intend to put their heart, mind and time into the business which may make the Seller feel more comfortable (as long as they like them!). This is ideal when the Seller does not have a key person that will stay on and run the business as the Buyer will take over their role.

Disadvantages

The Buyers in this case tend to be inexperienced in buying businesses so may not know what they are getting themselves into. Likewise, they may not have ever run a business and finding out this is not something you are good at once you have bought a business can be an issue! If the Buyer has no experience in this kind of business, then there will be a long training period and also uncertainty about whether the Buyer has an aptitude for this particular business.

Management Buy Outs (MBO)

Technically an MBO is where one or more of the existing management team that is already in the business finds funding and becomes the Buyer of the business and actually buys the shares from the existing owner. Sources of funds can be from them personally or their network as well as bank funding and deferred payments like the other Buyer types.

The process for an MBO is very similar to the other Buy types in that a process needs to be run for commercial negotiation, due diligence, contracts, post sale, etc. In fact, the need for an M&A Advisor to be a 'neutral but caring' third party to run the process and act as a go between can be even more pronounced. The reason for this is that long term relationships where the owner was the boss is now changing and people can have persistent underlying tensions which can come to the fore in this kind of process.

Without careful navigation, the deal can collapse with long term relationship damage. In the end, the goal is to build a model and post sale situation that both parties feel good about and it is important to understand the challenge that the change of roles and the impact of financial rebalancing and risk can have on both parties practically and emotionally.

Many Investor Buyer transactions (in fact almost all Private Equity) are in fact a form of MBO. Generally, the concept is that the PE firm is 'backing and funding' an existing management team. That team will get some kind of equity share to reap the future rewards of running and growing the business well. The advantage is that the PE firm will provide leadership, structure, help with business development, etc. which can often greatly accelerate success for the management team.

Advantages

The obvious advantage is that the management team already know how to run the business. The customers, suppliers, and employees are already working with them so this should make for an easy transition depending on the current level of involvement from the existing owner.

On the financial side, some businesses have a lot of excess cash that the owner just wants to get out in a tax efficient way and they are happy to take the risk with the management team so this is a great model. Sometimes the management team are family so legacy is being passed down in this way (although the use of Trusts is often more tax efficient). So there can be many situations where an MBO makes sense.

Disadvantages

Although an MBO seems like a logical model, there are two big drawbacks that mean this model is often not used in a pure sense (without an investor) in most cases.

The first is that the management team generally does not have the capital to put into the transaction. This means that they may need to take out a huge debt in the business plus have deferred payments to the Seller/owner so the business is stretched to the maximum. This creates huge pressure on the business and can even lead to bankruptcy if there is a market downturn. It also creates a huge risk for the Seller as they are relying on the deferred payments over potentially many years when they have no control to get the full payment.

The second issue is that most business owners have what we call Leadership X FACTOR. They are a certain type of person that is statistically a small percentage of the population that can successfully lead and grow business successfully over a long period of time. Generally, the management team that works in the business may be excellent at their jobs but are not this type of individual.

This is why the Private Equity model often works well as they have a sophisticated model and are able to fill this leadership void. Other Investor and Strategic Buyers may also have strategies to be able to replace the leadership void in different ways. In either case, this aspect of supervision, planning and leadership may allow the management team to flourish but with help so to speak.

Employee Ownership Trusts (EOT)

In this model the shares of the company are sold into a Trust owned by the employees (based on a percentage of their relative wages for example). Operationally this is similar to an MBO in that the Seller/Owner often leaves the business over time and the existing management team continues the day-to-day running of the business.

The difference is that the shares are sold into a Trust and strategic governance/strategic leadership is now with the Trustees.

Advantages

The operational advantage are similar to an MBO. The employees will continue to run the business day to day and the owner can transition out with no pressure from a Buyer as might exist in other models.

One of the big advantages is that for the Seller the proceeds from the sale are tax-free and they can sell the shares in the business to the Trust at an aggressive market rate. This can be especially helpful if there is significant excess cash which needs to be extracted from the business. The owner is then paid the balance out of profits until the sale price is met.

Also, the advantage to the employees is that they can receive a share of the profit once the owner is paid off. In fact, at the time of this writing, this can be in the form of a bonus of which £3,600 is tax free.

Disadvantages

As with an MBO, there is not a Buyer who is coming with funds so the sale is reliant on cash in the business, potentially debt and then a long deferred payment period which can create risk for the Seller.

For the employees, they do not get profit distribution until the Sellers deferred payments are made so this could be many years in the future.

Also, as with an MBO, the Seller who has been provided the X FACTOR Leadership to the business will now be leaving. This will be replaced by a board of Trustees comprised of a trained administrator, representatives from the employees and possibly outside expert people. This group will be responsible for guiding the business and leading the business. Often a board seat or some management involvement for the out going owner is promised but in many cases this still results in a significant loss of control and influence for the the Seller at a time when they really want to be leaving the business.

For some businesses that are well established, this can work well. For many others that have survived and thrived due to an X FACTOR owner/leader, this type of management structure will not be dynamic enough to keep to business moving forward and competitive. This, of course, creates risk for the Seller who is relying on this for the deferred payments for many years and many find the financial and legacy risk unacceptable.

The Leadership X FACTOR

We have found in working with the individuals that start, run and the navigate growth of successful companies that…they are simply amazing people!

Something like only 20% of companies make it to 5 years and 10% to 10 years. For the ones that do make it, the vast majority never exceed £1M turnover. So our clients are normally in a very small, elite percentage of people that can buck the statistics and navigate companies through the ups and downs and over a long period of time to create successful companies that someone else would want to buy (the topic of this book).

We have called the unique ability 'Leadership X Factor'. The reason this is important is that if they are going to leave the company this 'leadership void' needs to be replaced in some way.

We mention 'leadership' specifically as generally there are very good 'managers' in the business. This is a different type of person that is excellent at their day to day job but they are working under a Leadership X FACTOR person. Often, Leadership X FACTOR people will not work under others (not for very long) so the fact managers have been in place for a significant period often demonstrates they are not this type of personality. Often, the current managers could be mentored into Leadership X FACTOR type people but this would require a process and people from outside the company over a period of time and for the right type of person. It is not just something that just automatically happens any more than someone becoming a star football striker just because they have played on the team for a few years when the star striker leaves.

The reason understanding this is important in a business sale is that the 'leadership void' that will be left when the X FACTOR Leader leaves the company needs to be addressed in some way otherwise the business is likely to decline which has a significant impact on debt payments and deferred payments amongst other issues.

There are several ways in which we have seen this addressed that can work (in fact being in denial it is not an issue is the only real issue in our experience). For example, the Private Equity firms are very good at working with the existing management team to develop five year plans, hiring experienced support like CFO/COO around them, helping them with market acquisition and developing a strong non-exec board which may include a sector experienced Chairman for example. A trade buyer may simply leverage their existing leadership team (which is probably headed up by an X FACTOR Leader). An operator buyer may be an X FACTOR Leader in their own right with previous industry experience and track record.

In our observation, the important point is simply to recognise that this potential 'leadership void' (versus management) that may occur when the Seller leaves needs to be closely looked at and addressed as an integral part of the deal structure. And also to avoid the pitfall of thinking that, as a default, the day-to-day operating managers will be able to 'lead' the business without this void being addressed in some way.

Chapter 8

Getting Your Business
Ready to Sell

Selling a business can be one of the biggest activities someone undertakes in their lives, maybe third after getting married and having children! Often for a retirement sale, there is no hurry as the business has been going for many years or even decades, so the owner has a relaxed approach to timing.

In other cases, there are circumstances where the owner would like to sell as quickly as possible. Often these are due to the need to move to another country, health reasons, a change in the situation with a spouse or sometimes just a general feeling that the right time was a year ago and now it is time to get moving.

So, how is this process accelerated? In our experience, there are many factors that can both speed up the process as well as increase the likelihood of a business sale completing for the best value:

Good Books and Records

Having good books and records is one of the most important aspects of selling a business. Businesses are primarily valued on the ability to produce cash flow in the future and the Buyer needs to be confident that he understands the true profitability of the business. Without good books and records, it is very difficult to even come up with solid offers as there is uncertainty.

Often, we are left waiting for weeks and months before the accountant can get basic financials produced and then again get clean debtor books, stock takes and asset lists. Having all of this ready, clean and well-presented allows us to hit the ground running and can save months of time and instil confidence in Buyers that the systems are solid and the numbers they are looking at are accurate.

Implement and Document Business Processes

As we have discussed, businesses are like machines and the output is cash flow. As with any machine, it should run as efficiently as possible with the least amount of human intervention where possible. Good systems allow for a business to run smoother, staff to be moved around, better customer service and more repeatable processes.

The more that these systems and processes are working and documented, the more comfortable a Buyer will feel about taking on the business, scaling it, not being dependent on individuals, etc.

Create Redundancy For Whoever is Leaving (i.e. the retiring owner)

The Buyer needs to be confident that the business will continue to run as it has done in the past after the owner leaves. Any uncertainty in this area creates risk and risk pushes valuation and deal structures in a non-advantageous direction for the Seller. During viewings, one of the things Buyers like to hear is how much an owner plays golf or goes on holiday as it demonstrates the business is running fine without them. Usually, this is accomplished by building a team underneath the owner that slowly takes over running the business. Usually, a leader of this team is evident and can serve as the 'key person' that the Buyer will partner with and rely on to take the business forward.

Having a Realistic Expectation of Price and Deal Structure - Many weeks can be taken working with a Buyer only to come to the offer stage and realise that what they are willing to offer is not enough. For example, we often hear the objection that 'it is not enough to retire on' after having gone through a long process to get a Buyer to the offer stage.

Spending time and understanding what the business is really likely to sell for, the likely deal structure (transactions tend to have 3-6 components, see chapter on deal structure) and reconciling that with the Sellers expectations, in the beginning, can save a significant amount of time.

 This allows us to understand if we should even be proceeding with the business sale exercise in the first place (i.e. is it enough or does the owner need to keep working for a couple more years) and then be able to qualify a Buyer very quickly if they don't meet the financial criteria.

Having the Agreement of All of the Owners - Many businesses have more than one owner or have family members that need to agree to the sale. Having one owner spearhead the process only to find a Buyer, get an offer and have another set of criteria introduced by another owner or family member can greatly slow down or stop the process. The best thing is to involve all the stakeholders early on and have an agreement before moving forward.

Focus on the Due Diligence Phase - Across the industry, it is generally understood that about 75% of transactions fall through during the due diligence stage (after offers have been agreed upon). When the transaction falls through, it means another Buyer must be found and the process of getting to know them and getting offers repeated.

This obviously adds calendar time to the process. Therefore reducing the fall-through rate is a significant step in reducing the time to get to the finish line. The key to success in the due diligence phase is for the Seller to take it very seriously and do everything they can to produce documents in a timely manner, answer questions thoroughly and honestly and generally actively participate in the process regardless of the twists and turns.

This is one area where a good M&A Advisor can make all of the difference as they can manage the entire project. They will have a proven process for project management, control documents in the cloud, facilitate communication with all the parties and provide advice and guidance.

Assist the Buyer with the Funding Exercise - Most businesses are bought with some kind of commercial lending. Often, from a calendar perspective, this is one of the longest parts of the post Heads of Terms (HOT) being signed. The Buyer will need quite a bit of data from the Seller to give to the bank as well as feedback on questions and help with things like cash flow projections. If the Seller is able to give the Buyer timely assistance, this will greatly reduce the time for this step.

Instructing a Good Lawyer - A good lawyer means a) One who is very experienced with specifically business sales (property lawyers are generally not), b) has an attitude of working together with the other side and not as an adversary, c) has a relationship they wish to maintain with one or more of the parties meaning there is some level of priority d) they respect and will work with deadlines e) they will communicate regularly and return calls and emails f) they do not disappear for days or weeks with no explanation g) they are reasonably priced.

Lawyers that do not meet these criteria can greatly delay the sales process or even kill it at critical junctures. If you are working with a good M&A Advisor, they will have lawyers that fit all of these criteria which they have worked with in the past. We strongly advise not working with property lawyers just because you have worked with them in the past on real estate transactions as business sale transactions are fundamentally different.

Engaging a Good Sell-Side M&A Advisor - A good M&A Advisor is someone who has the experience of closing many transactions, realises the enormous responsibility of assisting someone to sell their biggest asset at a critical juncture in their life (and cares) and will have a well-developed process they can guide a Seller through to maximise the chances of selling and reduce the time.

The M&A Advisor will know how to assist with everything we have discussed above as well as be a guide on the journey with continuous advice and guidance along the way (think of a sherpa). The broker will also do 80% of the heavy lifting allowing the Seller to stay focused on running the business.

As always, we feel it is important that the M&A Advisor get paid when the Seller gets paid which is the day the business sells. We feel upfront fees (fees paid prior to sale) create the wrong motivations for the M&A Advisor and should be avoided.

If they are successful in general, the M&A Advisor's business model should have no problem accommodating doing projects at risk. A good M&A Advisor can streamline every process from packaging, finding Buyers, negotiating offers, due diligence and transaction management as well as bring all the right people in at the right time.

Willingness - One thing we find in business sales is that the old axiom 'where there is a will there's a way' is very accurate. We often talk about a 'willing Seller' and a 'willing Buyer' being the key ingredient to actually getting a business sale transaction over the line. The reason is that there are many obstacles along the way and compromises that must be made.

If both parties are willing, they will find ways to overcome these. As always, a good M&A Advisor will help facilitate the communication needed for this process. The business sales process is a team sport and if the team is motivated and willing, this can greatly increase the chances of success and reduce the time to get a transaction over the line.

CHAPTER 9

IF I SELL MY BUSINESS CAN IT SURVIVE WITHOUT ME?

Seller dependence is a question that is fundamental to both Buyer and Seller in a business sale transaction. From talking to many business owners, we find that over 70% do not feel that the business would be sustainable at its current level if they took over a month off, 30% would say less than a week. So how does a Seller hand their business over to a Buyer and move onto their retirement scenario without leaving the Buyer with a business that is compromised due to their departure'?

Buyer Perspective

As discussed previously, business valuation is largely around the business's ability to generate cash flow (return for the Buyer) in the future. If the owner is so integral to the business that their leaving is going to detriment this cash flow, clearly the business has less value unless they can be replaced in some form.

The Buyer also may be faced with customers, employees, suppliers and other relationships that feel let down as the business is no longer the same. This can also cause the Buyer to need to invest much more time in management and recovering the situation or hire expensive people to compensate further hindering the cash flow.

Seller Perspective

Sellers are usually concerned about legacy and leaving their customers, employees, suppliers and other relationships they have built over many years in good hands. If their leaving would cause a detrimental impact on some or all of these people, it can leave a bitter feeling about selling the business. Also, most transactions have deferred payments.

So if the business were to decline, often there are warranties that would cause a financial impact to the Seller in the form of reduced payments. Lastly, most Buyers are savvy enough to realise the owner is integral, many too integral, and will either value the business lower than the current cash flow might indicate or put strict warranties in place.

Why Do Buyers Want SME Companies Despite the Seller Dependence Challenge?

So one may ask, why should Buyers be so interested in the SME market place (generally under £50M turnover) if many of the businesses for sale involve a Seller who is retiring yet the business cannot thrive without them at the time the sale transaction is being discussed?

The answer of course lies in the fact that the cash flow from many of these businesses generates a 15%, 20%, 30%+ return for a Buyer. With well thought out M&A strategies such as implementing a strong non/exec board, hiring the right people and combining businesses together to achieve greater multiples, wealth can increase exponentially so it is worth the effort.

Further, although 80% of businesses in general do not make it to the 5 year point, businesses that have been around for 10 years plus often are so established with their approach, customers, locations, etc. as to be fairly low risk. In short, nothing in business is perfect and Seller dependence is just one of the aspects that needs to be overcome for Buyers that want to engage.

Overcoming Seller Dependence

There are several approaches to addressing this issue, short, medium and long term:

Seller stays on in the business for a short period of time during a handover period to the Buyer

This is the most common approach and generally 6 months is needed for a Seller to do the handover. This can take many forms depending on the business and usually involves a lot of time on the front end with a natural tailing off towards the back end.

Typically, the Seller either includes the handover in the sale price or is paid a market wage, often a day rate, during this period although this can be negotiated. The idea is for the Seller to do knowledge transfer, smooth relationships with customers and suppliers and provide a slow transition for employees and deal with any issues. This scenario of showing them the ropes is ideal if the Buyer intends to run the business themselves.

A new Managing Director is promoted from within

Often the Buyer does not intend to run the business and so someone else must be found. If someone exists in the organisation that is capable of being groomed for this position this is ideal as they already know the business, the customers and hopefully have the respect of the staff.

The challenge often is that in small companies if someone is of this calibre, they would not be working in that company for years but would have already moved on to move up somewhere else. But this depends on the Buyer. If they have infrastructure with other companies they own, it may just be that someone internally can be promoted to a version of a team leader or divisional manager role for the day to day running and the strategic activities are handled by the non-exec board.

The Buyer hires a new Managing Director to run the business

This approach can work if the right person can be identified. Often the Seller will help recruit this person and then the same approach as the above point is implemented. Because of the time to recruit, vet them during a probationary period and then hand over the time the Seller needs to stay in the business is generally increased.

The issue with this approach is that people hired from the outside often have challenges becoming the leader of a team that may have worked together for years. Also, often a salaried person may not have the same passion and drive as a business owner would.

The other challenge of this approach is there is now an extra salary consuming cash flow for a period of time as the Seller and the new person need to be paid which could impact valuation.

The Buyer uses management from another business

This approach is ideal if the Buyer has other similar businesses with senior management already in place. This is very much on a case by case basis but can be used in conjunction with the other approaches. Of course, the Buyer must be mindful of cultures and customer relationships and a detailed transition plan must be created but this can work well under the right circumstances.

The Seller stays on as a major accounts manager

Often the Seller has long standing relationships with the major customers of the business. Also, the Seller is sometimes actually happy to stay involved for an extended period albeit on a part time basis without all the pressures of running the business. A win/win approach for this can be that the Seller becomes a sort of major accounts manager with responsibilities for maintaining and growing strategic customer relationships.

They are generally well compensated for this and it allows them to stay involved in one of the most important aspects but with reduced responsibility and pressure. This can be used in conjunction with all the other approaches above.

Long-Term Approaches

Obviously the best scenario is that the Seller has created a business that no longer needs them present on a day/to/day basis so the sale process is actually relatively seamless. This takes time and generally goes through 4 phases of development:

1. Seller is doing almost all of the work (in the beginning) for all hours the day brings.

2. Seller gets help to do some of the work but the business still revolves around them and their expertise.

3. Other people are developed that actually run aspects of the business and the Seller moves more into working on the business rather than in the business.

4. The business runs fine without the Seller and in fact, often runs better.

The further along the business is on this continuum, generally, the easier the transition and often the higher the price the Seller can get for the business. Getting there is challenging and most small business owners never make it to 3 let alone 4 but it is worth bearing in mind as an objective to maximise the sale of the business in an eventual exit.

CHAPTER 10

WHAT MARKETING MATERIALS ARE NEEDED TO SELL A BUSINESS?

When selling a business it is obviously necessary to make people aware that it may be a good fit and want to buy it. Sometimes we liken the job of an M&A Advisor to a dating agency in the first instance, matching people together who may want to create a joint shared future in the form of a business sale/purchase. In order to communicate with these potential Buyers, materials must be prepared that describe the business at different stages of the process. There are many but I am going to describe the basic kinds of marketing materials we use for this process below:

Confidential Advertisements and Anonymous Teasers

At the start of the process, it is very important that the wider community does not know the business is for sale. Confidentiality is key to protecting relationships with employees, customers, suppliers, bankers, etc. who all might view the fact the business is for sale in a negative light and make decisions that could damage the business. However, in some form, it is necessary to let potential Buyers know the business is for sale.

For this reason, we create a confidential profile that describes the business generally but we are very careful to not include any information that would allow someone who knows the business to identify that this business specifically was for sale. This is very effective as a Buyer looking for a machine shop in South England will know they want something like that. If we add a general idea of the price of the business, revenue and profit and some key features they will know that it generally fits their acquisition profile and enquire.

The most common form is to create a 'teaser' which describes the business in more detail along with high-level financial headlines but does not reveal the identity nor provide enough information to do so. Teasers are generally used for proactive marketing to a target community as well as our networks.

Generally, we will prepare a target list of Trade Buyers and the Seller will approve each one before even a teaser will be sent out. This is to prevent any outreach to potential competitors, customers or just companies they don't like. For financial Buyers, the process is more straightforward as they are set up to review marketing material and are generally not known by the Seller.

Sometimes for our smaller clients, we use a simple web advert that will go out on the aggregators (Businsessforsale.com, Dalton, Rightbiz, etc) where people who are looking for business will scan based on certain criteria and enquire on businesses that look interesting. This is similar to using Rightmove or Zoopla if you want to look for a house. Our office gets over 50 enquires a week from this method and we probably screen 90% out but we meet some very good Buyers for certain types of businesses using this method.

Once a Buyer enquiries, we are very careful to first screen them to see if they are qualified and have a reason for wanting the business. If this screening is successful, we get them to sign a very strict Non-Disclosure Agreement or NDA (with financial penalties) which basically swears them to secrecy. We have remarkably few problems post-NDA so this is an effective process. Once the NDA is signed, we will generally send the Confidential Information Memorandum (CIM) as described below.

Confidential Information Memorandum (CIM)

CIM's are longer documents that go through all aspects of the business. This document has many different terms used for it depending on who is producing it like Confidential Business Review (CBR), Information Memorandum (IM), Business Overview, etc. but these are different names for the same thing. However, a CIM is not a prospectus, this is a specific type of document with legal implications often used for IPOs for example.

The CIM is typically 20-30 pages and has everything mentioned above plus much more detail about the owners, staff, customer base, facilities, market conditions, etc. The CIM attempts to answer every question a Buyer might have about a business before they ask which saves time and speeds up the sale process.

CIM's typically start with a questionnaire that is given to the Seller to fill in. A live interview is then done to make sure all the aspects are understood. Our CIM team will then create a draft which is further refined through an iterative process with the Seller.

Financial Pack

As we have discussed in a previous chapter, good books and records are one of the foundations for a successful sale process. We will generally ask for 3 years of historical filed accounts unabridged (generally only the abridged versions are on Companies House which doesn't have profit and loss) as well as management accounts since the end of the last financial year.

Management accounts normally come out of the accounting system and we are aware the balance sheets are generally not accurate as the accountant has not done adjustments. However, they are needed to make sure the company is still tracking at the same sales and profit levels since the last filing as well as a reality check on the balance sheet.

From these, we will prepare a recast which basically takes operating profit and adds back (generally increases) certain specified items to come up to a number we call adjusted operating profit or Adjusted EBITDA. This number is then often applied against a 'multiple' (see chapter on valuation). We can also use this information for other valuation methods including net cash flow (NCF), market cap or even an asset-based method.

We will also do a working capital analysis for the last 3 years. This is very helpful as it shows trends for cash, debtors, creditors and inventory. Also, when a Buyer makes an offer, it is generally based on the last filed balance sheet period if it is going to be a share sale (versus an asset sale).

Cost of Packaging

Packaging is critical in the business sale process in order to make sure the right Buyer and Seller get connected and the process is as efficient as possible. Putting packaging together takes skill, experience and time. Many business brokers will attempt to charge for this process. However, our view is that the other packaging items are part of the sale process and should not be charged for.

Generally, brokers and M&A Advisors will have templates that make this process very efficient and it is just a natural cost of sale in our view. For this reason, in our office, we typically do not charge for the CIM document as our only fees are based on the completion of a successful sale. (Often business brokers use the packaging process as a ploy to get large upfront fees and then make little effort to sell the business so the Seller should be wary.).

CHAPTER 11

THE BUSINESS SALE PROCESS

Selling a business is something most people will never do and for those who own a business, it is likely to be once or twice in their lifetime. Because of this the process of selling a business is not common knowledge but becomes incredibly important if you are the one selling what is probably your biggest asset.

This is why we often refer to the role of a Sell Side Merger & Acquisitions Advisor as a dating service in the beginning to match a Buyer and a Seller and then planning/project managing a wedding once the Buyer and Seller have reached the due diligence phase through to contracts.

In general, the steps to selling a business are:

1 - Instruction – The Seller needs to instruct the advisors to begin the process. The first instruction is normally with the M&A Advisor who will manage the packaging process and find Buyers.

2 - Packaging - During this step, an anonymous teaser is developed along with a Confidential Information Memorandum (CIM, although there are many names for it). There are many steps in this process, please see the chapter on packaging for more details.

3 - Buyer Search - If you are working with an M&A Advisor, they will do internal matching within their existing Buyer network as well as their research databases which tell them who is in a similar sector and/or might be buying this type of company.

They also may do direct marketing to potential Buyers. This is typically done with the anonymous advert or teaser using a tool like Linked In so the people enquiring do not know the identity of the businesses. Once an enquiry is made, the Buyer signs an extensive NDA before the company is disclosed and they receive the CIM. For trade Buyers, it is typical for the Seller to have an exclusion list of companies they do not want to be contacted.

4 - Buyer Screening - Depending on the type of reach out, there could be many people who respond. These people will need to be qualified to make sure they are a good fit in terms of finances, location, background, do they really want something like this, timescales, etc. We generally screen out 75% of the people who respond so our business Sellers only deal with the top 25% at this stage.

5 - Viewing - Once the Buyer had a look at the CIM, we would normally have another conversation with them to determine if the business would be a good fit. If so, we would schedule a Zoom call or an in-person meeting with the Seller.

As confidentiality is key, if this were in person this would normally be after hours or sometimes offsite. We normally say business sales are 40% head and 60% heart, so this is a good opportunity for Buyer and Seller to see if they vibe with each other and for the Buyer to get a much clearer picture of the business. We would not talk about commercials or even go into much detail on financials in this meeting, it is more about seeing if there is a potentially good fit and chemistry so to speak.

6 - Financial Review - If the Buyer decided they like the business (heart), we would then schedule a session to really go through the numbers (head). This will help them understand the cash flows in particular which will drive the offer.

7 - Offer and Acceptance - Once the Buyer understands the cash flow, they should be in a position to make an offer which, of course, will be subject to due diligence, financing, getting leases transferred, etc. In other words, this step is really just making sure that everyone is on the same page with the commercial framework before we put in the tremendous amount of work that comes with the next steps.

8 - Heads of Terms (HOT) or Letter of Intent (LOI) – The Buyer and Seller may go back and forth a few times but once they agree on a framework typically we get both parties to sign a HOT or LOI which lays out the commercial terms and normally locks in exclusivity for a period of time.

There are often abortive charges in this document if one of the parties pulls out of the process before the expiry of the exclusivity period without a good reason, the other is libel for any professional fees incurred.

9 - Financial Due Diligence (FDD) - The Buyer will produce a list of items they want to see (usually a drains up on all aspects of the business) and also activities they want to do. This list will be placed usually in a Cloud Due Diligence locker that the Seller can access to place the documents and we can project manage the list to completion. We will normally set up a weekly all hands call to review progress as well as send reports out to all parties to keep the project on track.

10 - Working Capital and Excess Cash Confirmation – Usually at some point during Financial Due Diligence a somewhat tense, drawn-out discussion will take place with the parties accountants involved over what the minimal level of working capital is, adjustments to what costs are for the business versus the Seller personally which ends up in a calculation for what excess cash will go to the owner at closing. Please see the separate chapter which discusses this.

11 - Funding - Most businesses are bought with some kind of commercial lending so the Seller will need to work with the Buyer to get the information that the funder needs. The type of funding sought will determine the level of complexity. Asset-backed lending (i.e. debtor book or equipment) is the most straightforward whereas cash flow term loans can be complex. This step can take the longest,t so it is important that it is started early.

12 - Post Sale Planning – During due diligence, many areas around post-closing will also need to be addressed like constructing a 3-5 year financial model, the expected working situation and compensation for the Seller, new contracts for the staff, etc.

This is a time for the key person or people that are going to be staying to build a relationship with the Buyer as it is likely they will be working together for some years. Note that only the key staff need to be involved in this process in a very confidential way as generally the Seller should not inform the vast majority of their staff until after closing day.

13 - Other Due Diligence – As part of the due diligence process there will be many contractual relationships the Seller has such as Leases, Licenses, Debt Transfer, Strategic Contracts, Franchise Agreements, etc. that will need to be transferred to the Buyer that will need to be looked at individually and addressed.

A good example is a lease where we will need to understand what the landlord will need to agree to the sale. There are also banking relationships, relationships with supplies and of course the franchisor will generally have first right of refusal so they need to be notified and there will probably be a fee due.

14 - Legal Due Diligence (LDD) – The process is similar to Financial Due Diligence except the list is generally provided by the Buyer's legal council. Also, the Seller staff will populate the Cloud data rooms with responses but these are typically not opened for the Buyer to view until the Seller's lawyer has given the ok.

15 - Business Sale Contracts - Once all parties agree due diligence is complete and funding has been secured, we will review the financial offer and make any tweaks based on things that have come up during the process. Once this is agreed upon, the next step is to instruct the lawyer to start preparing the contracts.

Typically, we use a Share Purchase Agreement (SPA) for the purchase of the shares of a Limited Company or an Asset Purchase Agreement (APA) for the purchase of just the assets and goodwill. However, there are many more documents the lawyers need to create around the lease, consultancy agreements for post-sale, shareholder agreements, Board Minutes, forms for Companies House appointing new directors and changing ownerships, etc.

The lawyers will generally communicate with each other, but it is very important to project manage the process in our experience if the parties want to complete the transaction in a timely manner. This is because the lawyer will need many inputs from the Buyer, the Seller, accountants, brokers, the landlord, etc. and any delay in information can delay the process.

16 - Closing - For the most basic format, all parties get together with the lawyers and the documents to sign in a room and sign the paperwork and the Buyer transfers the closing payment to the lawyer's escrow account. The lawyer then does the appropriate transfer of funds to the advisors and whoever else is part of escrow, the balance going to the Seller.

 Often there is a celebration of some sort, usually paid for by the M&A Advisor! It is also possible for the lawyers to facilitate this process remotely using a tool like DocuSign if the geography of the parties does not allow for this.

17 - Post Closing - Generally there is a review of the closing accounts after about 60 days if that method for working capital allocation was opted for. Often the closing payment is split up and a portion is retained until this calculation is complete. Adjustments are made based on differences in working capital (see the previous chapter) and any other financial differences. At this time a review of the business Seller's participation in the business can be undertaken and any adjustments made.

So, as you can see, there are many complexities in getting through the process of selling a business. We normally say that it is 5x more complex than selling a house but fortunately, most people only need to do it once or maybe a couple of times in their lifetimes!

Why Engage a Sell-Side M&A Advisor?

You can see why many people engage an experienced Sell-Side M&A Advisor to manage this process. The process can be very time-consuming and having someone that has the systems in place plus does this every day so has many experiences to call upon can take away 80% of the hassle factor from the Seller.

A good M&A Advisor will also help mitigate any people issues and act as the go-between for any negotiations, so the Buyer and Seller never have to fall out over money (easily done) as well as manage a timeline.

Our suggestion is that Sellers should never pay upfront fees to a business broker as the motivation to go through the significant amount of work the next 8.2 months+ will entail is mitigated as the broker has a significant portion of his payment upfront.

CHAPTER 12

CONFIDENTIALITY MATTERS

When most people decide to sell a major asset like a house or a car there is generally an advertising process to make as many people aware the item is for sale as possible. This can even include putting a for sale sign in front of the house or a notice inside the car windshield for example.

In the case of selling a business, this community advertising approach would have many negative consequences. Because of this, the normal advice is to tell as few people as possible the business is for sale and only reach out anonymously. The following are some of the groups and reasons for this anonymity:

Customers - If customers know you are selling they might make many negative assumptions like there is a problem with the business and better to find another supplier as quality might go down, etc. They could lose money if you suddenly go out of business and they have outstanding orders, deposits or you are about to become unreliable, etc.

Suppliers - Similarly, some suppliers are strategic and may look for other outlets in your area. Also, they could try and poach staff or modify payment terms if they think there is a financial risk.

Employees - This is generally the last group you want to know your business is for sale. In fact, we recommend not telling the employees until after the sale is made. The reason is that many business sales fall through and this can create all kinds of problems with staff morale.

Just knowing a business is for sale can make people insecure and they will start looking for other jobs. After the sale is complete, this is a different story as we can generally position the Buyer as an investor and tell the story about how everything is now going to be bigger and better, etc.

Competitors - Clearly if a competitor knows your business is for sale this is generally detrimental as they can use this against you with customers, they can poach employees and also go after strategic supplier relationships.

Family members - Often business owners do not share the fact they are for sale with family members. One reason is that a family member can potentially let the cat out of the bag (often inadvertently) with all of the above people.

There can also be a lot of fear and uncertainty with certain family members which may not be helpful. Children also need to be treated with caution as they will often socialise with other children of companies in the above categories and inadvertently let slip the business is for sale.

Staying Confidential

There are 4 ways that we make sure that a business sale stays confidential:

1. Generic Teasers - We make all teasers that would be used for outreach anonymous with the specific company not identifiable. These teasers must be approved by the Seller to make sure there are no small clues someone who knew their business could pick up on. A good example is how long they have been in business or some feature or tagline that is specific to them. Another step is that a teaser will only be sent to the companies or groups of companies that the Seller specifically identifies as being 'safe'.

2. Signed NDAs - Any Buyers whom we are going to supply the Confidential Information Memorandum (CIM) and reveal the company's name must sign a strict Non-Disclosure Agreement (NDA). This explicitly states that they are not allowed to share even the fact this business is for sale with anyone else. We have remarkably few problems with this happening once an NDA is signed.

3. Culture - The third way of keeping everything confidential is to create a culture where everyone understands how important this is. Within a good business M&A Advisory practice, this will mean everyone from the receptionist to the managing director will have had training around how important this is and ways of preventing any problems.

For example, it is essential that no one in the office tells their children about the businesses that the office has for sale. Children talk to other children in the community and one small comment at a social event can cause the fact the business is for sale to spread like wildfire.

4. Controlled Site Visits - Site visits can be challenging as staff may wonder who these people they don't recognise are. For this reason, we generally limit site visits if the staff that are not meant to know about the sale are present.

If we do need to go on-site, we normally try to go after hours and/or construct a cover story so as not to arouse suspicion. Often Buyers and Sellers will meet in person at the M&A Advisors office or a local hotel/restaurant or even at the Seller's house to avoid detection.

Confidentiality is critical in a business sale and is something that the Seller deserves as their ongoing business should not be impacted by the business sale process. With the proper training, policies, procedures and culture 99% of the time any issues with confidentiality can be avoided.

Chapter 13

Working with Advisors

Selling a business is one of the biggest challenges a person may undertake in their life next to getting married and having children. It may also be one of the most complex, yet most people who own businesses only do this once or maybe twice in their careers. Due to this, working with professionals that specialise in the business sale process can make the business sale journey a lot less stressful with a better outcome.

Selling a business is a team sport which needs a group of strong professionals to support clients during the process. The following are advisors that generally make up the team on the Sellers side:

Sell Side M&A Advisor – Sort of the quarterback that coordinates the process from beginning to end, finds the Buyers through an extensive prrocess, structures the transaction, supports the client's interests and keeps everyone together and calm when things get stressful and brings the champagne on closing day!

Business Lawyer – Their main role is to draft the legal contracts once due diligence is complete, the main document usually being the Share Purchase Agreement and about 15 other ancillary documents. They will also typically perform legal due diligence and may even be asked to advise on the Heads of Terms early in the process.

Personal Lawyer – These can be the same but are often different as the personal lawyer can advise the Seller as an individual shareholder. This is common when more than one person owns the shares. They can also assist with any post-sale consultancy contracts, share schemes or employment.

Accountant – The accountant is generally the incumbent accountant who initially is responsible for producing historical accounts. They will generally be asked to produce management accounts up to the current period and assist with a 3-5 year projection.

They are needed throughout the process to answer accounting queries and assist the Seller with personal tax matters. They will also review the SPA to make sure the numbers are correct and generally manage the closing account process.

Personal Financial Planner – Generally a large amount of money is being paid to the Seller at closing which will need to be invested and optimised for tax purposes. The Financial Planner can work with the Seller to develop a comprehensive investment strategy for the Seller and their family that maximises returns and minimises tax.

Tax Advisor – They will work with the accountant and wealth manager on any business or personal tax matters relating to the transaction.

Property Lawyer – If the business has freehold properties, usually a de-merger of the property out of the company being sold is executed which requires specialist assistance.

Which Advisor?

There are many different advisors that will be happy to have the project work. The following are a few basic principles that will help a Seller choose the right one:

Education and Qualification - Experience and education is very important, the business sale process is very complex. It takes on average 9 months to sell a business and there are many accounting, legal and functional challenges along the way.

Due to this, the advisor must be very knowledgeable to be able to guide the Seller during the process. Ideally, the advisor will have the appropriate professional qualifications. But at the very least, they should have several years of experience and many transactions under their belt.

Reputable Firm With a Significant Track Record - Like with everything in the business world, a successful firm will have developed policies and practices over time to optimise the service they offer. Business sales is a team sport with many different players so a larger firm will have a deep bench so to speak. They will also have a management hierarchy the Seller can access should issues arise.

Dedicated Advisor - Although the Seller will want to work with an organisation as above, it is important that there is one point person that they trust that is the main point of contact. A business sale process is very involved and can take many months so continuity is important. The Seller should interview this person and decide that they can trust them to guide them on this journey.

Success Fee Only for Sell-Side M&A Advisor- Our view is it is very unhealthy to pay upfront fees for the M&A Advisor role. The advisor should get paid when the client gets paid. Upfront fees can become a profit centre in themselves for many firms and the corporate culture slides into a lack of focus on getting the handwork done to get the transaction over the line.

What Role Does the M&A Advisor Play?

Pricing and Packaging - The advisor will work with the Seller to create both anonymous and more detailed marketing documents to give to potential Buyers. This will include a financial pack that helps a Buyer understand their financial situation as well as commentary to understand the business.

As part of this process, the advisor will work with the Seller on pricing strategies. Although business transactions are normally a collection of components, it is helpful to express this as a single, order of magnitude value in many cases.

Identifying Buyers - The advisor will then use a variety of methods to find qualified Buyers for the Seller to engage with. These include working through their own networks in the first instance and using an in-house Buyer search team for targeted Buyer searches. They will then screen Buyers to make sure they match the Seller's criteria before doing an initial meeting with the Seller.

Negotiating Commercial Terms - We have discovered that the quickest way for people not to like each other is to talk about money and particularly the value of their business. Due to this, it is much more efficient for commercial discussions to be done through the advisor.

These kinds of transactions are very complex and this allows the advisor time to work with the Buyer on the offers, then taking time to explain thoroughly the offers to the Seller and then work with the Seller on counter offers. This is done one on one so there is little emotion or need for defensiveness and allows a process to take place which is mostly about financial engineering.

Project Management - Once the Buyer and Seller have agreed on terms, there will be many weeks of due diligence, funding activities, legal, post sale, planning, etc. It is the advisor's job to create and manage a plan for this including regular meetings and updates with Buyer and Seller.

Business Broker or Mergers and Acquisitions (M&A) Advisor?

Business brokers tend to work on smaller transactions, often on the high street. One way to look at it is that Business Brokers generally sit somewhere between property agents and M&A Advisors. Property agents are not trained to deal with an asset that is producing cash flow and all the ramifications that go with that so a business broker is required. However, business brokers are generally not trained or experienced in all the anomalies with funding, tax planning, complex equity structures, etc. that go with the larger transactions.

M&A Advisors can work on transactions up into the billions and with public companies so this is, on the face of it, a broad category. Generally, the M&A Advisors that work with smaller businesses are in a segment called Medium Sized Enterprises (SME).

Generally the more experienced, better trained and certified the advisor is, the more effective they will be as with most other things in the world of business. M&A Advisors tend to have more training and should have engaged in significant education as well as gained certifications as a demonstration. Many of them started off as brokers early in their careers so also have more experience.

This is just a general guideline, who the Seller works with largely comes down to an individual preference for a specific firm or person.

Can a Seller Just Sell The Business Without Help?

The answer to this question is yes of course. As with all things in life, you could also service your own car, do your own plumbing and file your own taxes. But does it really save any money? When you have a very complex transaction with many moving parts over nine to twelve months, what are the chances the average person is going to engineer the best, multi-dimensional deal structure on the first go? Where are you going to find the buyers? Also, no one has exact figures but we estimate that 80% of businesses that go up for sale never sell (most without advisor help). This number may be somewhat skewed by High Street businesses which can be harder to sell but it makes the point that this is a challenging activity with no guarantee of a result.

The following are the challenges that you as a Seller would need to overcome:

Pricing/Commercial - How do you know what your business is worth? Transactions are not just a number, they have many facets...how do you balance them all to get the most out of your business sale? Even one aspect missed could cost you £100Ks.

Finding Buyers - Where would you find Buyers? The average person has very limited networks and no access to advanced databases that identify potential buyers as an M&A Advisor should. Anyone can advertise on the public websites but we estimate only 1 in 10 enquiries are qualified, do you have time to sift through these? How do you know which ones are qualified in the first place?

Confidentiality - You don't want employees, customers, suppliers, etc to find out the business is for sale. Are you able to operate in this covert way over many months on your own?

Negotiation - People that might otherwise like each other fall out and become offended when discussing money (think prenups, the couple would almost never discuss these themselves and still think the wedding was happening, they would let the lawyers do this). There is a process to mitigate this that has been developed over many years (and mistakes), obviously, an individual doing this for the first time has no access to this. Mistakes in this area can be very costly, can you afford them?

Transactions are also complex with closing payments, deferred payments, earn-outs, stock rollover, penalty clauses, warranties, etc. Many things have to be balanced together, do you want to take the time to understand all of this and are you willing to live with rookie mistakes? (Note: there is generally a lot of money involved so even small mistakes are expensive).

Project Management - There are many things to do over many months including due diligence handling, funding, legal, post-sale planning, etc. All of these have to come together to get a transaction over the line. Do you want to have to learn what all of these are and if so, do you really want to have to manage all of them?

It can become a full-time job for 6 months and distract you from running your business. Once you get to close, you may say sales are down because you were too preoccupied with the business sale and find the Buyer is willing to pay less, the advisor fees may have been a fraction of this reduction!

A Friend To Take the Journey With You - A good M&A advisor is like a Sherpa guiding you up to the top of the mountain. They should have extensive networks and access to advanced buyer databases. They should be experienced in running the negotiation, due diligence, contracts, etc process guiding the process to avoid all the potential pitfalls. They are a confidant that will walk with you and share their experience and expertise every step of the way...they are someone to talk to.

If you hit a problem even they cannot help with, they will have colleagues that can...so you will not walk alone. Selling a business can be very emotional, so this kind of support can be invaluable.

CHAPTER 14

THE EMOTIONAL SIDE OF

SELLING A BUSINESS

We always say that buying a business is 60% heart and 40% head. This is to try and explain the different processes that go on in the Buyer's mind. Most of us are familiar with buying a house and the need to feel like you 'want it' at a gut level. But then it has to work from a financial point of view in terms of deposits and payments, proximity to work and school and considerations like whether it is a good investment, etc. which is the head part.

However, there is often a very emotional experience that is going on for many Sellers simultaneously which I will describe below:

Loss of a Comfortable Identity - Many Sellers have spent years and decades devoting their life to building a business. This has been a huge part of who they are as a person, in the community and within their family. Letting go of this can create many emotions and sometimes a sense of wondering who they are or are going to be.

Life is all about change starting from when we were born and growing up, and this is just another step in the process. The important thing is to realise that these kinds of feelings are very normal and most people report after a year or so that an entirely new world and sense of purpose and belonging has opened up once they have free time to develop other interests.

Will it Be Enough Money? - We hear this question come up all the time and it is a very logical one (head) but can also create enormous amounts of fear and anxiety (heart). The Seller is transferring their biggest asset as well as the vehicle that has supported them and their family for many years. The answer to this question is important and very real.

Our advice is to work with a well-qualified personal financial planner who can work through a plan as well as the numbers. This has the effect of answering this question clearly as well as moving it from a fear into a concrete plan of action with tangible measurements and outcomes.

You Can't Stay Here Every Day (says the partner) - Often couples have been so busy raising children and building the business that they have not spent extended time together other than holidays (again often with children).

Sometimes there are unresolved issues that have been pushed under the carpet for years behind this facade of activity. Suddenly, with the sale of a business both of them will be together on a daily basis and this makes one or both of them very uncomfortable. We have seen people unconsciously kill deals to avoid this happening.

The problem is that at some point this has to be worked through as everyone will want to retire at some stage. At least being aware that there may be issues will allow them to look at it squarely and possibly seek some kind of help to talk through the issues this life transition may bring up.

What Will I Do With the Money? - This may seem like a nice problem to have but it causes people a lot of anxiety. Many Sellers have spent their lives being very good at what they do and have no idea about the wider world of investing or financial management. And of course, everyone has an opinion, most of them tend to be uninformed and out of date. Our suggestion is to find a certified financial planner who specialises in working with people in exactly this situation.

As I have discussed, selling a business is a team sport which requires having the right advisors for the right job to ensure a smooth process (i.e. lawyer, accountant, business broker, etc.). A personal financial planner is really just another part of the team that handles this aspect post sale and ongoing.

There are many, many more options for investment than most people realise. A professional that specialises in this will area will be able to help with understanding these, especially as they relate to tax and cash flow.

I am Worried About My Staff - Most good business owners have a keen loyalty to the people that have taken the journey with them and helped them build the company...we applaud this on many levels. Staff should be taken care of if at all possible and this is in the Buyer's best interest as it is generally the people that are instrumental in creating the value in the business.

The important thing here is to find a Buyer that the Seller is comfortable with and has a plan that feels right. This should be one of the red lines for the Seller before they will proceed with the transaction. Beyond that, there is always the possibility that the Seller can share some of the proceeds with key workers and that the Buyer can offer incentives for people that stay. The key to this is seeing that it is important and focusing on it early to make sure everyone is on the same page.

I Want My Customers to Be Well Looked After - As with the previous point, the customers are a fundamental aspect of what has made the business successful. Almost every Buyer is also going to be very keen the customers feel well looked after and continue to buy from the company. However, are they able to run the company in a way that this is likely to happen? This is a question that has to be asked during due diligence and if the Seller feels there are issues, they have every right to pull out of the transaction.

At a practical level, most transactions involve deferred payments over 2-5 years so the Seller has to be confident the Buyer will be able to run the business successfully. Also, it is very common for Sellers to stay involved with customer management for an extended period as a sort of outside account executive. This allows the Seller to keep tabs on things and leverage relationships that have been built over many years.

The key aspect to the emotional side of selling a business is to realise that there is a very emotional side to selling a business and that this is both normal and ok. However, it is very important to acknowledge these emotions and work through them in a constructive way.

Otherwise, the old saying 'whatever is repressed gets expressed' is never more accurate as it can manifest as irrational behaviour that can cause transactions to fail. On the other hand, emotions that are dealt with out in the open and constructively provide enormous opportunities for personal growth during this process.

CHAPTER 15

BUILDING A TRUSTING RELATIONSHIP WITH THE BUYER

We have often likened the role of the Sell Side M&A Advisor to a dating agency in the first instance where we use our packaging skills and networks to match potential Buyers and Sellers. As we have discussed previously, we find this process is 60% heart and 40% head.

Once a Buyer and Seller decide there is the potential for a transaction, it becomes more like project managing a wedding. There are two sides, natural tension and different expectations that have to be managed but there is a common goal for a joyous event at the end...and it is usually very important that everyone is still friends on closing day.

The process of the Buyer and Seller getting to know each other, due diligence, contract negotiation, post sale planning and exit planning is very multifaceted and generally takes many weeks and many hours of discussions, analysis, soul searching and often compromises.

Along the way, there are many areas where the Buyer won't know all the information and will have to take a leap of faith that revenue will be maintained at current levels or the employees and customers will stay for example.

The Seller has to take a leap of faith in things like whether the customers and employees will be taken care of and indeed whether any post sale payments will be made in a timely fashion. There will be many times in the process when the Buyer and Seller will need to overcome obstacles, come up with creative solutions and often solve complex problems together.

The Need For Honesty and Transparency When Selling a Business

All of this activity has one key ingredient that smooths the way: **Trust**.

When people trust each other and feel that it is a joint venture, our experience is that most issues that arise can be overcome. 'Where there is a will there's a way' is never truer than in business sales. When people don't trust each other, every little hiccup becomes fodder for the next conspiracy theory and a downward spiral begins. So building and maintaining trust is absolutely crucial throughout the process.

One of the key things to understand about trust is that it can take weeks and months to build and a split second to disintegrate. There are many things that can cause this to happen including people not doing what they say they are going to, being late to meetings, rudeness and arrogance, breaking confidentiality, bloody-mindedness when solving problems and just generally people's personalities clashing.

But there is one sure instant killer of trust which is usually permanently fatal in a business sale:

Dishonesty.

Once dishonesty is discovered, generally trust collapses. One of the big reasons for this is that now the other party has no idea if anything they have been told is true...everything is under suspicion. The other party also wonders what other areas of their life the dishonest person is using this approach and how they may come to bear on the business (i.e. lying to the bank or government about another business which could cause financial issues when discovered).

For this reason, our advice during a business sale process is to be transparent about everything. This is for two main reasons:

- The first is that the business sale process is a long, in-depth process where people really get to know each other. In fact, during due diligence, both parties are basically doing a drains up analysis of each other personally and commercially. So we have a view that everybody is going to know everything eventually so you might as well be honest about it.
- Secondly, honesty builds trust and we just discussed how powerful trust is in the successful completion of a business sale process. It may feel uncomfortable to share certain things at the time, but the other person sees that and respects you for being honest. Over time, they begin to trust everything you say and do and problems are solved much more quickly.

Often I have Sellers (and Buyers) ask for my advice on how they should 'position' some negative aspect if it comes up. My advice is always the same...**be honest and be yourself.** They are going to find out anyway and if they feel you are sugarcoating or creating an artificial facade, it erodes trust...it isn't worth it.

Most successful business owners are very impressive people (only 10% of companies make it to 10 years in the UK for example) and Buyers understand there are positives and negatives and just want the truth.

The Seller needs to remember that the Buyer is only looking at your business, contemplating paying £MMs, and dedicating time to operating the business post sale because they inherently respect what you have done and can't do it themselves.

CHAPTER 16

WHAT ABOUT COMMERCIAL PROPERTY?

Many businesses have commercial property (s) that is owned by the business. This can be the office the business is run from, a factory or warehouse used by the business or even an investment property not related to business operations.

One way commercial property can be looked at is profit that the owner did not take out as dividends but invested in commercial property inside the business. This would not be that different than if they had invested in stocks/bonds on the balance sheet instead of taking dividends. An argument can then be made that this 'frozen' profit should therefore be returned to the owner at closing in a similar way to excess cash.

Alternatively, if the property is appropriate and functional for the business, it can be viewed as any other cash producing asset such as a machine which drives EBITDA and is, therefore, part of the balance sheet delivered to the Buyer at closing.

There are generally two ways of dealing with this commercial property:

1 - The Property is Removed (Demerged) from the Company Prior to Sale and Rent is Added

This is the most common scenario as most business Buyers do not want to buy real estate. An exception can arise if the property is a small office of not much value for example. (The reason is that buying a property takes cash for the deposit (i.e. 25%) and the returns are far less than buying businesses). The Buyer would often prefer that the property is removed from the business prior to the sale.

The issue arises that removing the business generally creates a Stamp Duty charge as the property would conventionally be 'sold' to the Seller personally or another Seller company. This tax can be significant so the Seller will want to avoid it. The solution is a 'demerger' where the property is moved into another company in the group which is then moved or demerged out of the group. This requires a specialist lawyer and HMRC approval and a certain lead time but is a very common approach.

When the property is taken out of the company generally this will create a rent requirement that the company must now pay to the new owner (the Seller personally or his new limited property company). This was a cost that was not on the P&L previously and therefore reduces EBITDA which will likely have an impact on valuation and also on the available cash flow post sale. So an evaluation must be done about whether the reduction in valuation is offset by the value of the property being taken out to make it worth it so to speak.

2 - The Property is Left In the Business

If the property is left in the business it would seem at first glance that there is nothing to do as it becomes part of the asset base that generates cash flow and the value is reflected in EBITDA and the valuation. However, this is not necessarily the case as often the property value (bought with the owner's profit) far exceeds the value of the cash flow being created.

In this case, a common approach is to determine the market rent value and also the market value of the property generally through a survey (often 2 or 3). The rent would then be subtracted from EBITDA rolling through to a lower valuation but then the property value would be added back into the valuation.

Another way to visualise this is if the property was not part of operations at all but a pure investment and was staying in the business it would clearly be the owner's profit that would be in addition to any goodwill value.

Part of the contract package at closing would include a long-term lease on the property to the Seller's company. This often benefits the Seller as ironically the property can actually go up in value now that it has a long-term lease with the company being sold!

Additional Considerations

Property often has a mortgage attached to it. So it is important that these calculations are done net of the mortgage of course as this is the actual Seller equity in the property.

Often the mortgage can be used as part of the debt financing package for the business. If there is no mortgage, generally the Buyer can get quite a large loan against the property (i.e. 75%) if it is staying in the business and this becomes part of the funding package.

There can be other issues with a property that needs to be considered like any liens that might exist, government mandates that might be due/coming in the future, changes in the tax regime and/or zoning, etc.

Chapter 17

What to Expect Post Sale

Once the deal is closed there is a sense of relief more than anything. The last couple of weeks can be intense as all the details come together and everyone just needs a break. However, this is where the next phase begins as announcements need to be made to the staff, banking relationships changed, customers are informed, and a new management structure is potentially implemented to name a few.

Telling the Staff -This can be one of the more nerve-racking steps in the process. There should be a good plan for what the messaging is going to be and a decision about whether the Buyer is going to be there. Often it is best to announce that an investor has become involved as the expectation is that the company will be growing. This puts everyone at ease as the leadership they are accustomed to is not leaving at least at that point. Key staff will often have bonuses related to the acquisition and usually, these should be discussed with them separately.

Transferring Bank Authority - The Buyer needs to take control of the bank and credit facilities but this can take quite some time (sometimes months). Unfortunately, this step can generally not be taken until the day after closing (in case the deal does not close). Due to this, it is important to make a plan with the Seller to make sure that payments and bank transactions are continued until the transfer.

Informing Customers - The process for this will vary from company to company and between different customers. The guiding principle here is to use common sense and not take any steps that might cause customers to seek to do business elsewhere. Again, the investor versus business sale angle can be used, the Seller can inform the customers personally or a general announcement can be sent out. Again, the guiding principle should be what will instil customer confidence.

A Modified Management Structure - This will generally be implemented in some form. It is important to get the buy-in from key people, document any changes and be clear on any new reporting requirements. The rule of thumb is to take this slowly to allow people to adjust and develop a positive attitude about the acquisition.

The Hand Over

Often the owner will have an active role in the business during a transition period. The goals and plan for the transition period should be well documented during the post sale planning phase in parallel to the due diligence process. The handover process can take many forms depending on the company but the goal should be continuity and the least disruption possible, particularly around customer service.

Many owners will take a more focused role after the handover, the most common being some business development responsibility for the major accounts they have relationships with. This allows the owner to stay involved and make a tangible contribution to the company as long as they are willing.

Generally, the transition period is planned to last for around 6 months. In practice, there is a certain momentum and it happens a lot faster. This is particularly the case if existing staff are taking over leadership roles. In that case, often the owner finds themselves sort of written out of the script and stepping back much quicker than the 6 month period.

CHAPTER 18
WHAT IF I AM NOT QUITE READY TO SELL?

Planning to sell your business may be one of the most important things you do for yourself, your staff and your customers and others involved with the business. There are many aspects to exit planning that will probably require several specialist advisors to assist you. The aim is not to make you an expert in each of these areas but to give you enough information to have intelligent conversations with the advisors and make informed decisions.

For business owners who want to exit their business within the next 1-2 years, it is important that they start the business sale process now as it can take a year to sell a business (or more) and then another 6-12 months to actually exit.

For those who want to exit in 3 years or more, there is time to make changes to the business and their own personal wealth and tax situations to put them in the best place possible when they actually go to market.

The potential areas they can focus on are:

- Sales & Profit Acceleration
- Business Optimisation
- Personal Financial Planning
- Tax Planning

Sales & Profit Acceleration

Business valuation is generally based on profitability which in turn is often driven by increasing sales. Small increases in profit can lead to 300%/400%/500%+ of the increased profit as it manifests in the business valuation calculations. Also, a growing business is much more attractive to a Buyer and will put upward pressure on valuations.

However, how to get there is often a mystery for many business owners.

Revenue growth tends to be a result of a successful strategy, the right people and a formal sales process. Profit growth tends to be a result of putting in better systems and understanding what product lines and processes are profitable, optimising costs and streamlining processes.

All of this is greatly enabled by better systems, reporting, KPI development and management restructuring.

Generally, outside assistance from a specialist is invaluable both in terms of broad knowledge, transformation strategies and coaching.

Business Optimisation

Most businesses have evolved their systems organically over a long period of time. Often they are focused on a few key people or maybe just the owner is heavily involved in day-to-day activities.

One of the main core objectives of organisational optimisation is to allow the owner or key people to create systems, both physical and automated, that allow them to take a step back somewhat from the business and allow it to function without them, even if for limited periods. This is essential in an exit situation as the Buyer will want to know these people can exit and the business can keep running.

Another core objective is to introduce systems that increase revenue and margin and reduce costs. All of these lead to more profit. More profit leads to a higher business valuation and generally a smoother running company which of course is more attractive to a Buyer.

Many businesses often have less than optimal capital structures which can be consolidated and optimised (i.e. expensive loans and leases, poor credit terms, etc). They may also need capital in order to drive revenue/profit growth as part of the Exit Plan. Looking at the capital structures and financial plan as early as possible will support the Exit Plan goals and make the business more attractive to a Buyer.

Personal Financial Planning

Selling a business is probably the largest item most people will ever sell with a sum of money being paid to them at one time that may exceed all their other investments. Managing this large sum of money both in terms of investment potential, tax planning, retirement planning and inheritance becomes absolutely critical.

The different areas of personal financial planning that need to be addressed tend to be:

Investment Potential - Making sure the money is invested with the right return/risk profile. This may be the largest amount of money a Seller has ever had at one time so understanding where to put that amount of money takes planning and generally professional advice.

Tax Planning- Working out how to minimise tax with money coming out of the business sale as well as inheritance, investment income, pensions, etc.

Retirement Planning - Making use of available instruments such as pensions and investments to ensure the money paid is efficient in retirement. A Seller should also have a feeling for how much they need to retire which may impact how much they need to sell the business for and how the cash flows work out.

Inheritance Planning - Making sure the money ends up in the right hands with the lowest tax upon passing.

Becoming educated on these aspects to enable active participation with the appropriate wealth advisors is critical to the best outcome.

More on Tax Planning

Selling a business generally creates a tremendous opportunity to pay tax as the monies involved are so significant or a tremendous opportunity to optimise tax with the right advice and strategies.

Although on the surface the tax situation around selling a business looks relatively straightforward, it can get complicated very quickly and needs the right advice from an accountant and wealth manager and decent planning.

For example, as a baseline, the business sale will generally be subject to Capital Gains Tax (CGT) of generally 20% as the base rate. However, currently Business Asset Disposal Relief (formerly called Entrepreneurs Relief) allows for a 10% tax on the first £1m for each shareholder. Additionally, often excess cash in the business and directors' loans can be added into this equation so they only attract CGT. This can be a very tax efficient way of getting the accumulated profits out of the business versus dividends which can attract much higher tax rates.

Then there is the matter of property in the business being extracted and SDLT, share rollovers, Trusts and investment strategies for the large sums that are paid at closing, EIS schemes, Employee Ownership Trusts (EOT), and many more.

Doing planning early with a comprehensive strategy is essential. There are many different strategies so being somewhat educated in these areas to at least reality-check the advisors is important.

Getting the right advisors to assist with this and also becoming educated in order to participate with the advisors is important.

Chapter 19

Pitfalls to Avoid

This chapter covers the situations we have learned through hard experiences delay or kill transactions completely. Business sale transactions are time-consuming, expensive and completing them is important (as the owner often has an appointment with the beach!) so making an effort to understand and avoid or mitigate these issues early on can make all of the difference.

Choosing the Wrong Sell-Side M&A Advisor

The Sell Side M&A Advisor will generally manage the process from beginning to end so if they are weak in any one or multiple areas it can significantly compromise the process. This starts off with the ability to search, screen and introduce appropriate Buyer candidates right through to managing due diligence and then the contracts phase.

They should also act as a sounding board for the Seller to help them through difficult patches. They need to be savvy enough to help navigate the many twists and turns in the process otherwise the Seller may be on their own or at the mercy of friends and family who have an opinion but generally little experience. So choosing the right Advisor to begin with is probably one of the most important decisions in the process.

Lawyer Issues

The process of working through an M&A transaction is much more like a wedding where two parties are coming together for the same mutually beneficial event, with a natural tension between both families and some pre-nuptials. The problem is that most lawyers are trained and geared toward managing a divorce and do not understand that an adversarial approach in an M&A transaction may kill what was actually a good deal for both people.

A good M&A lawyer will understand this and hold ground on important points but always have the bigger picture and respectful relationship that needs to exist between Buyer and Seller in mind. Due to this, it is very important to choose a lawyer with significant M&A experience and avoid lawyers that are mainly property oriented.

The other issue we find with lawyers is that they tend to take on too much work and if your transaction is a small one and they have no outside connection, your project may get pushed to a lower priority. Due to this, it is often helpful to choose a lawyer that regularly does work for the M&A Advisor or has some other connection to someone you know where performance on your transaction will have a good or bad wider impact on that relationship.

Accountant Issues

Accountants are vital team members during an M&A transaction. The Seller's accountant will need to produce historical reports as well as assist with future projects and validate the commercial framework and advise on tax issues. The first issue arises when the accountant is very slow to produce these reports and the project team is left waiting in limbo until they do. This is a difficult problem to solve and up to the Seller to put pressure on them to meet deadlines or consider hiring an outside M&A accountant to help with the transaction.

The other issue with accountants is that they often have very little training and exposure to key aspects of an M&A transaction. The first is that they do not really deal in 'risk'. For example, few people would ask their accountant which stock to buy on the stock market, this is intuitive.

Yet risk runs through the M&A paradigm, driving everything from business valuations to payment terms and interest rates.

They also generally don't view the world through the personal situation of their clients (i.e. that the client needs to retire for personal reasons and it is not just about financial calculations). Most accountants also have little formal training in business valuation which is a different skill set than traditional accounting as it is forward looking, unlike most accounting which is about looking backwards.

Because of this, they will often be very negative on M&A transactions as they see their client losing a cash flow they have been enjoying for years and from their lense not understanding why they would give that up for what they consider to be a low sale price. However, our experience is that most accountants have their clients' best interests in mind and their opinion is important and worth considering but it should also be taken with a grain of salt for the reasons above.

Poor Books and Records

Poor books and records are one of the main reasons that the due diligence phase ends up in the transaction not continuing. At a high level, the Buyer is buying future cash flow and they need to be able to rely on all the different elements that make up that cash flow.

We normally work with 3 years of filed accounts which the accountant would have prepared and we would expect them to be accurate. We then work with management accounts out of the Sellers accounting systems since the last filed accounts. This allows the Buyer to see that the business is on track in the most recent months. So if this basic reporting is not available, it makes it very difficult for a Buyer to get comfortable and almost impossible to get commercial lending.

Beyond that, specific areas that tend to cause problems are debtor books, stock and work in progress. Debtor books which are inaccurate (i.e. don't reflect who owes the company money) have a knock-on effect to the P&L

and Balance sheet (i.e. if a debtor isn't real, the sale didn't really happen). Also, if many debtors are over 90 days, questions arise as to whether the sales related to them were real.

Also, the stock must be accurate for the obvious reason that this may be one of the biggest items on the balance sheet. But also, for the less obvious reason that incorrect stock impacts the Cost of Sale figure on the P&L which then can have a direct effect on EBITDA which then has an impact on the valuation. The same goes for the Work in Progress figure, anomalies translate directly to EBITDA in most cases.

Dishonesty

The Buyer is going to spend what could be £MMs of pounds on a business and rely on the future cash flows generated by the customer base and serviced by the employees and processes of the business. If what they are looking at turns out to not be true, some could be ruined. Because of this, a Buyer will also be evaluating whether they can have confidence in what they are looking at.

If they feel that the Seller or someone working on the Sellers team is being dishonest, this confidence can evaporate as well as their willingness to do the transaction. Our advice is to be honest in everything as it builds trust. Also, to have the idea that over many months everything will be found out anyway so there is no use being dishonest and better to deal with the truth. People respect each other that way and trust and respect are what get deals over the line.

Not Building Trust with the Buyer and Seller

This is related to the above point about dishonesty. Generally, the Buyer is going to take many things on faith to gain the confidence necessary to be willing to spend ££MMs on a business purchase. He will need to build trust in the business, customers, staff, process, etc to reach this level of confidence.

We always say that trust is what closes deals as there are always 2 or 3 things that come at the end that require both parties to compromise and take leaps of faith…the amount of trust that has been built during the process is directly related to how willing they will be to do this.

Landlord and Premise Lease Issues

Many businesses have premises that are required for them to operate which are rented or leased. When a business is sold, many of these leases have conditions about changes in ownership and or personal guarantees that need to be transferred. Often, the leases have to be renegotiated with the landlord's legal council. The issue is that this whole process can be slow, tedious and time-consuming.

Usually, it is what it is and needs to be done if the Buyer wants to stay on the same premises. But having these negotiations is often left late in the process and ends up delaying the whole business sale. So the advice we give is to consider this a critical path item and to start this stream of work early knowing it could go very slowly, especially if the landlord is an institution in our experience.

Partnership Issues

Many businesses are owned by more than one person. However, often one person has a significant majority so is used to calling the shots. This majority shareholder is usually the one that initiates the business sale and is most involved in the process. Occasionally, when a significant amount of work has been done one of the minority shareholders decides that they are not in favour of the sale for some reason.

Most shareholder agreements have drag along/tag along provisions which would mean, in theory, they can be forced to go along with the transaction but this can be costly and time-consuming. Therefore, it is usually prudent to make sure all of the shareholders are on board with the business sale before the process starts or be prepared early to deal with any legal action to force the transaction through if necessary.

Not Really Ready to Sell

In an earlier chapter, we discussed the 'switch' that needs to go off inside of a Seller letting them know it is time to move on. This is just an analogy but it demonstrates the idea that the Seller has to have some level of really wanting to sell their business.

If they are just lukewarm, they are unlikely to make the compromises necessary and put up with the multi-month headache that is generally the business sale process. As the process itself is such an investment for both Buyer and Seller, it is important that the Seller be sure early on that this is something they want to do.

Unreasonable Financial Expectations

The Seller has a right to want whatever they want for their business, no one should judge that as it is their asset. However, this may be more than is reasonably possible for any Buyer and more importantly, any lending institution. If the Seller's expectations are above what will work from a valuation, cash flow and lending perspective, the transaction will almost certainly cease when this is discovered. Again, as there is so much investment in a business sale transaction by both the Buyer and Seller, it is very important to evaluate this as early as possible.

Lack of Timely Follow Up

Business sale transactions take a lot of focus from both Buyer and Seller who are often paying outside professionals to be part of the process. There is also just a natural pace and a certain energy level everyone devotes to it with an expectation of completing it in a reasonable time period.

If one side is very slow on responses, it can greatly affect the costs on the other side as well as focus. At some point, the other side may just give up and they will not see the transaction ever completed and move to another Buyer or Seller they think they can get a result with. Business sales should not be a pressure cooker as they go on for many months and people would become exhausted. They should however move at a reasonable pace with each side responding in a timely manner to keep the process going.

Declining Financial Results

This results when the Buyer engaged the transaction with financial results from a previous period and may have even had up-to-date management accounts when the Heads of Terms were signed. However, over the several months that due diligence/funding has run, the financial results have declined. This is obviously concerning for a Buyer as they are buying future cash flow which will often be determined by the run rate of the business at closing.

In this situation, the reason for the decline needs to be determined. If it is a one-off and temporary, there are measures that can be taken to keep the deal on track but sharing the risk should continue. If it is deemed to be permanent, then the transaction may need to be renegotiated or terminated.

Lack of Cash

Lack of cash at closing can occur for several reasons. All of these are problematic as they can result in the Seller not getting their entire closing payment, the business not having enough cash to run, long-term debt not being paid off, etc. The main reason this arises is that the debtors have not paid at their normal rate which could be a fluke or because sales are down just before closing or the commercial lending is less than expected.

Often the teams are surprised when this happens at the last minute. To mitigate this, very careful cash flow planning should be done at least a month before closing and monitored very, very closely until the day of closing. Contingent plans should be put in place if there is any chance an issue could arise.

Bank Issues

There are many bank issues that can hold up a transaction. These can be a transfer of any loans with the change of ownership, the Buyer's lender nitpicking and taking forever to approve the lend for the transaction, releasing the mortgage on properties, the bank approving the transfer of credit lines and invoice financing, liens being removed from the company at Companies House (we have seen debt that was paid decades ago still not cleared in the public record), etc. These are all issues that have to be dealt with for a transaction to complete. The mitigation is to identify them early and start the process knowing the speed of the bank is a limiting factor.

Government Issues

There are many issues I am grouping into a category called 'government' that can stall or stop a transaction. Everything from business licensing issues, personal licensing requirements, zoning and permits. But also outstanding legal issues and fines, back taxes, unresolved government court cases and investigations, etc. As always, mitigation is done by identifying these early and assessing the likelihood of resolution before too much cost is incurred in the process.

Funding

No list of pitfalls would be complete without mentioning how many issues the attempt for the Buyer to secure funding can cause. The commercial lenders can be very tedious in their requests, demand audits, take illogical positions...and then disappear for long periods. Unfortunately, commercial lending is necessary for most business sale transactions so working through it is necessary. Our advice is for the Buyer to engage a specialist lending agent to assist in this process and stress test the lending as early as possible to make sure the transaction is viable.

Chapter 20

Next Steps

Selling your business may be one of the biggest things you do in your lifetime next to getting married and having children. It often ushers you into a whole new life, one you probably deserve for all the hard work put into getting the business where it is today.

You should look to get the most out of the process and most often engaging a professional who has the experience and training as a Sell Side M&A Advisor can make a big difference. I wrote this book as I want to be that person (with my team and company of course) for a number of people who read this.

I feel it is our vocation to help people who are ready to retire, those who 'the switch' has gone off, to sell their businesses and move on to whatever adventures life has in store next.

If you are looking to sell your business and exit, we would love to help get you started.

Please feel free to contact me at:

Transworld M&A Advisors UK

KGorman@transworldukmanda.co.uk

Whatever direction you go in, we wish you well on your business sale journey!